THE LIFECYCLE TRADE

HOW TO WIN AT TRADING IPOs AND
SUPER GROWTH STOCKS

Eve Boboch | Kathy Donnelly | Eric Krull | Kurt Daill

ISBN Print 978-1-7335066-0-1

ISBN eBook 978-1-7335066-1-8

Cover and interior design by Michelle Feingold, owner, founder, and art director of MDash, LLC. For more information, please visit www.behance.net/michellefeingold or email mdashllc@gmail.com.

Contents

Acknowledgments

The authors would like to acknowledge several people who have shared their wealth of trading experience over the years and taught us many great lessons. Much appreciation and thanks to the following mentors: William O'Neil, Jim Roppel, Dr. Brett Steenbarger, Dan Zanger, and Peter Brandt. The importance of mentors can never be overstated. We are forever grateful for the selfless way these individuals have shared their time and wisdom.

We would like to acknowledge our friend and colleague Ajay Jani for sharing his intermediate term sell rule with us and granting permission to use the rule in our research study.

A special thank you to our very talented editor, Kelli Christiansen, for her creativity and working her magic with words to help us bring out the best in our manuscript.

Our amazing designer, Michelle Feingold, is a true artist that has brought our book to life, and we thank her for setting the gold standard in finance book design.

We sincerely thank all of our reviewers, especially John Boik, Peter Brandt, Mike Cintolo, Michelle Feingold, Ajay Jani, Jim Roppel, Jack Schwager, Dr. Brett Steenbarger, Ryan Worch, and Dan Zanger, for their constructive feedback and valuable comments, which were of great help in systematically improving our final manuscript.

We also want to thank TradeStation's Michael Burke, Don Pratl, and Chris Walker for their support and assistance with the TradeStation platform that was used to produce all of the charts and graphs.

Finally, much love to our families for being supportive of our endeavors over the past few years as we searched for a method to discover the next Amazon.

Foreword

I have had the honor of knowing each of the authors of *The Lifecycle Trade* for almost fifteen years. I've enjoyed meeting with this group every January to discuss their views on the market for the coming year, and their insight is always outstanding. Their collective experience in studying, analyzing, and researching the lifecycle of growth stocks and IPOs is thorough and incredibly valuable for even the most veteran traders looking for the next monster stock. Their ideas are fantastic, and the bottom line is this: They have made money for my hedge fund partners and me.

Handled properly, just a few big winning IPOs can dramatically change your career and your life—and this book will help you in that pursuit. The IPO market is treacherous, but it presents opportunities for exceptional gains. *The Lifecycle Trade* provides a detailed overview of the IPO lifecycle as well as wisdom found in new rules for reducing risk and locking in profits. The insights on the odds of successfully profiting from a monster IPO and the effects of drawdowns are enlightening. The MCP Holding Method (Figure 8.1) should be posted on every trader's desk. It will be super helpful for even the most experienced traders. And, the Q&A near the end is invaluable.

After thirty years of managing money, this book has opened my eyes to new ideas and made me realize that there is always more to learn. It has reminded me that trading requires discipline and hard work. I hope *The Lifecycle Trade* will help you stay disciplined while you find the next Amazon.

—Cheers,
Jim Roppel

Meet the Research Team

 **Eve Boboch** has been a portfolio manager and market strategist at Roppel Capital Management since 2011. Prior to joining the firm, Eve enjoyed a multifaceted career at the Federal Reserve for more than twenty years. She earned an MBA in Finance from Loyola University of Chicago. She started investing in 1995, learning from mentors, including William O'Neil, Jim Roppel, Dr. Brett Steenbarger, Peter Brandt, Dan Zanger, and the study team members. She has a passion for the stock market and stock analysis and is featured in the book *How to Make Money in Stocks Success Stories* by Amy Smith.

 **Kathy Donnelly** received a degree in Electrical Engineering from the University of Houston. Despite a successful career in the Oil and Gas industry, Kathy's goal has long been to manage her own money. It was in 2006 when she met her team members in Naperville, Illinois, and was able to fulfill her dream and start trading actively. Today Kathy manages her own money while pursuing fitness goals. She recently became an Ironman and is currently training for her second race. Her mentors include the study team members, William O'Neil, and Dan Zanger.

 **Eric Krull** has been a full-time trader since 1999 and has managed a hedge fund in the Chicago area since 2013. Prior to that, he was a business management consultant, financial analyst, and project engineer. He earned an MBA from the University of Chicago with a concentration in Investments. Eric develops TradeStation programs to analyze markets, stocks, and trading strategies. His mentors include William O'Neil, Jim Roppel, Dan Zanger, Mark Minervini, and the other study team members.

 **Kurt Daill** is a full-time commercial airline pilot and part-time money manager and stock speculator. He served as a Top Gun Instructor and U.S. Naval Officer for more than twenty years. In furtherance of his investing career, Kurt started reading books by William O'Neil in 2003. In 2014, he founded the Pilot Investors Group, LLC, which coordinates monthly training events for individual stock speculators. Kurt remains engaged in the process of striving to become an expert in the field of money management and stock speculation.

INTRODUCTION

ANYTHING IS POSSIBLE in the stock market. Disciplined traders understand this and do everything they can to be prepared for unexpected events. They know that stocks can soar sky-high one day and plummet the next; such is the nature of trading. They also understand that there is no reward without risk, no matter what they're trading.

That said, seasoned investors also know the highs and lows of trading *initial public offerings*[1] (IPOs) and growth stocks. Dealing in these securities can be exhilarating, challenging, and rewarding. Is it worth the risk? It certainly can be, especially if we understand the market, if we are prepared for the unexpected, and if we can take the lows as well as the highs.

How the Journey Will Unfold

First, we assume you are an experienced trader, at least to some extent. Perhaps you have been trading successfully for several years and are looking to learn more about how to trade exciting but volatile growth stocks. Or possibly you have a good working knowledge of trading and want to learn how we discover and profit from future

---

[1] The first time we use some new terms we developed as part of the study, as well as other trading terminology that may warrant explanation, we boldface and italicize the term and include a definition in Appendix I.

big winners shortly after their debut as public companies. Either way, we assume the reader has a working knowledge of trading concepts and stock charts, as well as technical analysis experience.

No matter your reasons for joining us on this journey, we'll share how we navigate stocks early in their lifecycle and, hopefully, avoid some costly mistakes: We have made plenty of missteps in our quest to successfully trade growth stocks soon after they went public, and we think others will benefit from what we've learned.

We'll start with discussing why it's important to study the lifecycle of growth stocks in the first place. We'll cover how IPOs evolve over time into mature stocks, focusing on observations made during our in-depth study. We'll share with you the patterns we identified that cover most new stocks and what rules we use to buy and sell them. Finally, we'll share with you our results along with various rules we've created from our collective experience.

In other words, we'll share a complete methodology to handle these potentially lucrative situations—navigating market peaks and valleys, trading rules, and even the results of our detailed study of IPOs dating back to the early 1980s, which were enlightening and bolstered our own trading performance.

Indeed, we coauthors are experienced traders with a passion for research. Our studies have provided illuminating information about the lifecycle of **Super Growth Stocks**, which are stocks that have proven themselves to be exceptional investments (increasing 100 to 900 percent or more) in transformative companies with accelerating growth. With that, we'll look at the stock patterns we discovered that help us determine where a stock is in its lifecycle. We'll look at common mistakes and how to avoid them. And, we'll share how to identify tradeable patterns as well as how to craft and apply strategies, and some factors that can help discover the next high-performance stock. Let's start with a quick look at some of these big winners.

CHAPTER 1
IN SEARCH OF THE
NEXT AMAZON

AMAZON WENT PUBLIC at $18 per share with a valuation of $438 million. Since then, the market capitalization has increased to an astounding $1 trillion at a recent peak. Amazon has returned lucky early investors with an amazing increase in its stock price of more than 90,000 percent since its IPO in 1997 to 2018 (see Figure 1.1).[2] Yes, you read that right: ninety thousand percent! Tesla delighted investors who purchased shares in 2013 with a move from the $30s to a peak near $390 in just over four years. Netflix has a market capitalization of more than $145 billion vs. $309 million at the time of its IPO in 2002.[3]

These awe-inspiring stocks, and others like them, have soared since their IPOs.[4] The potential return of such life-changing investments is alluring to say the least. What if there were an edge to trade and profit from the next Amazon, Tesla, or Netflix? What if there were a way to spot the big winners early? What if select sell rules could provide an advantage? What if we could avoid some of the pitfalls of trading stocks early in their lifecycle?

---

[2] As of 10-22-2018.
[3] Market capitalization numbers are as of the time of this writing.
[4] A recent industry trend to watch is startup unicorns or private companies with valuation of more than $1 billion (e.g., Uber, Airbnb, SpaceX). When these unicorns go public, some of the growth in value has occurred prior to their public debut; this can have implications on the magnitude of growth rates post-IPO.

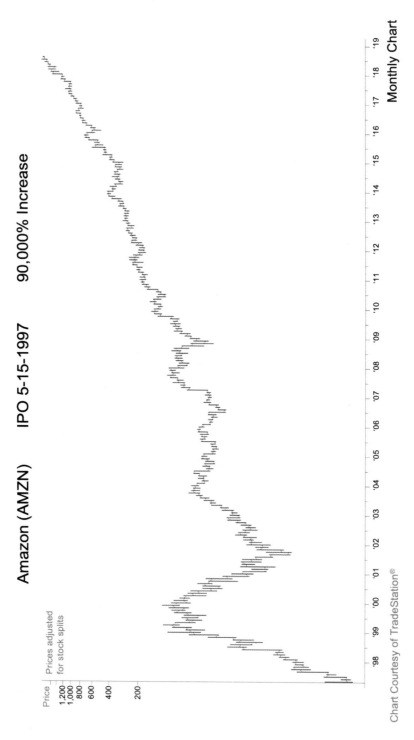

Figure 1.1 Amazon Monthly Chart

Chart Courtesy of TradeStation®

We asked ourselves exactly these questions and then undertook some research to find the answers. The results of that research can be found in this book, which will reveal a methodology to identify tradeable patterns early and implement buy, hold, and sell strategies to profit from the next Amazon. In these pages, you will find the patterns we discovered, which we have named *lifecycle patterns*, as well as other research findings that have helped us more successfully trade stocks soon after their IPOs.

Nothing worth having comes without risk. We believe that the conclusions from our years of study demonstrate how stocks behave during their lifecycle, providing an edge when trading more volatile and sometimes treacherous growth stocks. It takes discipline, passion, hard work, and determination to put the findings into practice. As traders, the findings have helped us to manage the risks involved with trading growth stocks throughout their various phases and to profit from what we've dubbed the *lifecycle trade*. Next we share our personal experiences on why we wanted to study IPOs.

Thoughts From the Research Team
Super Growth Stock Study: Why Study IPOs?

Q: Why did you embark upon a multiyear project to study IPOs and Super Growth Stocks?

A: Eve—I wanted to see if there was a way to identify a potential big winner (such as Amazon, Netflix, Tesla, and eBay) prior to its run. Over the years, I had earned mixed results in trading IPOs, often making fast, substantial profits and then giving back gains as the stock corrected.

Eric—I wanted to do the study because I was hoping to find factors that were common amongst the most successful stocks of all time. Then, by using these factors, I would be able to identify new potential big winners and invest in them before the big move would begin. I noticed that some of the best winning stocks in any given year were stocks that recently went public—and I had been missing them. Or, sometimes I knew about a stock, but I had been afraid to invest in it because of my past mishandling of IPO stocks during their initial volatile trading periods. I wanted to stop missing the winners and conquer the fear of trading recent IPOs.

Kathy—I knew I needed to become more rigorous in my trading. In some ways, I was very lucky when I started my trading career: I was able to buy stocks and hold them for a long period of time. For the past few years, however, the market has been very choppy. I didn't really change my trading style, and I was still trying to hold everything forever, which was not a good solution. I ended up losing more money than I should have. Since it's rare to find a stock that you can buy and hold for a long time, it finally sunk in that I needed to adjust my sell rules. It also became very apparent that any long hold is rare. A trader must be very selective and therefore needs strong rules for the majority of stocks, not just the minority.

Kurt—I *round-tripped* a trade in Visa shortly after it went public. After having a reasonable gain, I gave back all the profits. I did not think much of it, other than being frustrated with not retaining any gains. I should have recognized this round-trip as trading tuition and looked deeper for lessons learned. Years later, I traded Alibaba, also shortly after it went public, and had a significant gain (30 percent). Unfortunately, my Alibaba trade became a carbon copy of my Visa experience. Recognizing that I had been taken to school again trading in a new market offering, I knew I needed to get involved with the study to learn how to handle these newer issues properly.

How IPOs Grow Up

Amazon, Tesla, Netflix, Google, Facebook, and others like them have shared the same trajectory: private to public to Super Growth Stock. These are rare jewels. Since many stocks tend to perform poorly, we wanted to find a way to home-in on the elite performers. In studying the charts, we noticed that specific patterns develop over time, beginning shortly after a company goes public.

We believe that the majority of new issues, with few exceptions, go through defined price patterns. These price patterns are caused by the transition in ownership from private to public investors and large institutions. As these institutions research a company's potential, the shares of a stock move from the hands of venture capitalists, founders, and short-term traders to longer-term investors. This common trajectory creates defined patterns.

Traders typically have a mental picture of what a normal price pattern of a successful IPO stock looks like. Google is the perfect example of what investors are usually looking for. The *base* was short (eighteen days) and shallow (13 percent). Since this *consolidation* occurred shortly after the stock's debut, we call this an *IPO base*. The stock proceeded to move up quickly (more than 100 percent in forty days) with power, never undercutting the initial IPO structure. (Google is a needle in a haystack: This type of price action is rare and difficult to find see Figure 1.2).

Another great example of an *initial base* formation is Amazon (see Figure 1.3). Notice the strong price move right out of the gate as Amazon starts its amazing run.

The reality is that most newly public companies go through a kind of *IPO disease*. A new issue that exhibits IPO disease might pop and have an initial great run up that quickly fails (with the drop more than giving back the entire rally) or just immediately fizzle and die after its first few trading days. If the stock does come back to lead, it can take a long time.

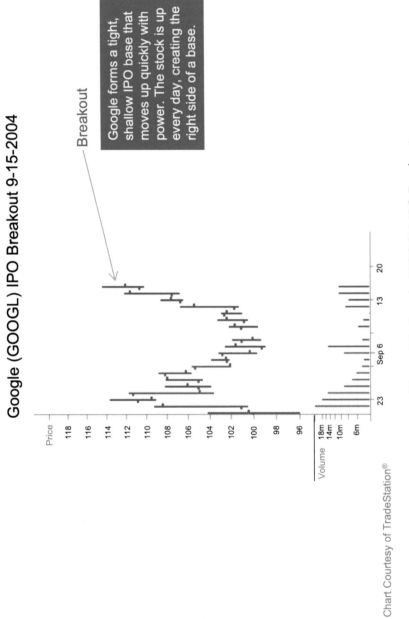

Figure 1.2 Google (GOOGL) IPO Breakout

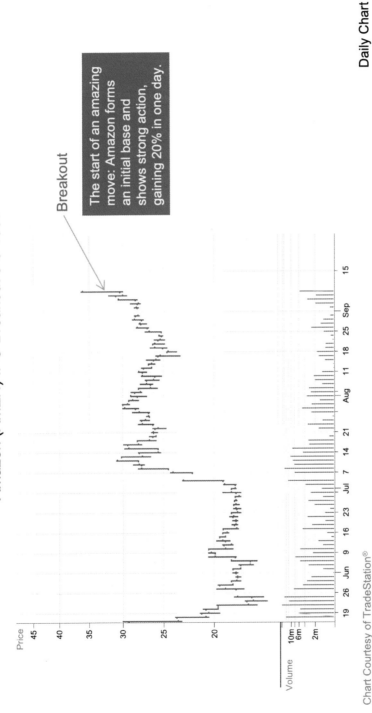

Amazon (AMZN) IPO Breakout 9-8-1997

Breakout

The start of an amazing move: Amazon forms an initial base and shows strong action, gaining 20% in one day.

Daily Chart

Chart Courtesy of TradeStation®

Figure 1.3 Amazon (AMZN) IPO Breakout

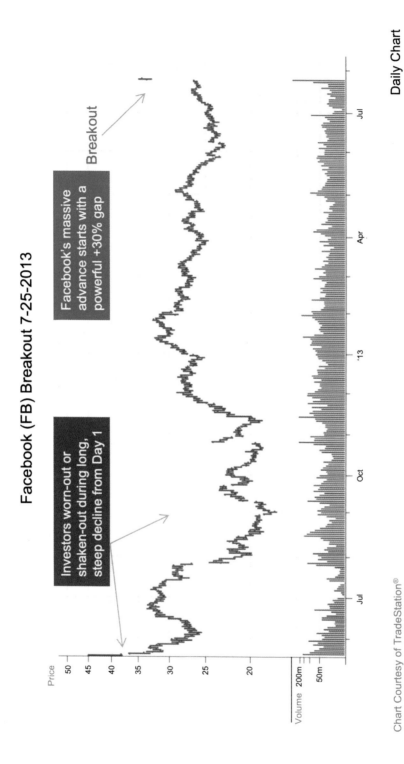

Figure 1.4 Facebook (FB) Breakout

Some IPOs don't even have an initial rally. Remember Facebook just prior to its IPO? Everyone appeared to be a fan, and the media heavily covered the issue with a positive bias, therefore exhibiting multiple contrarian warning signs. True to form, it opened at $38 and quickly tanked to $18 in a few months. Over time, Facebook came back and went on to become a Super Growth Stock; however, investors who jumped in immediately were hurt financially as the stock initially dropped in price (see Figure 1.4).

Of course, not all stocks suffer from IPO disease. After looking at many charts of the best-performing stocks of the past forty years, we started to see similar price patterns occurring over and over again. In the chapters to follow, we'll share the patterns and explain how the findings will help find once disease-ridden IPOs that turn into big winners. And we'll explain how our analysis shows why these companies should never completely fall off the radar.

CHAPTER 2
SUPER GROWTH STOCKS STUDY

LET'S TAKE A BRIEF LOOK at how we conducted the study to set the stage for the findings. Honestly, the first phase of the study was a bit of a bust. The original objective of the study was to discover key traits exhibited by top-performing stocks at the beginning of their runs in order to assist in successfully identifying and trading future big winners. We wanted to determine the most important factors that help flag a potential future leading stock including fundamental factors, such as past earnings, sales, market capitalization, return on equity, margins, etc., that predict success. We found that to be nearly impossible, however, since data were either missing or inconsistent between sources. So we took a different approach.

Study Methodology and Findings

After finding that our original approach didn't accomplish what we'd hoped for, we decided to focus on reviewing charts of the best-performing stocks of all time. It reminded us of a story about chimpanzees.

It goes something like this: Jane Goodall began studying chimps in Tanzania in 1960 without any college training or research plan. She thought the best way to learn about them was to live in the jungle with a family of chimpanzees and to interact with them and observe their behaviors. Her research was original and was considered groundbreaking. The moral of the story: The best way to learn about chimps is to spend a lot of time watching chimps.

That's what we did for our study. We had not seen any in-depth books specifically about IPOs or about the lifecycle patterns of stocks. So, we watched the chimps—or, in this case, the best stocks that went on to be elite performers. We spent a lot of time studying just how the best stocks behave during their lifecycles and examining what the charts looked like after their IPOs as well as before and during their big moves. After we pored over the charts, we were surprised to find several recurring patterns, which we mapped out, named, and defined into what we call lifecycle patterns.

We believed the patterns would help us learn how to handle various types of price moves during these stocks' lifecycles. As we became more familiar with the patterns, we realized we had created a new trading language that would help us trade IPOs and more mature Super Growth Stocks.

After we categorized the stocks, a question popped into our discussions: What type of sell rules would make big profits? We chose a select group of high-performance stocks for testing to determine how sell rules performed. We also determined which rules worked better on certain lifecycle patterns, and we'll share those findings as well.

In the second phase of the study, we examined many stocks that went public since the 1980s and are still traded today. We analyzed the stocks in order to determine how much they have gained, how quickly they have moved, and how large their corrections have been.

This review confirmed that the majority of new issues going public, with few exceptions, go through defined price patterns and phases. We realized that stocks, like living beings, start young, and then, hopefully, grow up. This is part of a stock's lifecycle. Now that we've shared how the study was conducted, let's dive in to the *lifecycle phases* of stocks to see how it provides a framework for our methodology.

CHAPTER 3
SUPER GROWTH STOCK LIFECYCLE

AFTER ANALYZING THE DATA collected for our study, we found that it was possible to map the complete *Super Growth Stock Lifecycle*. An IPO is a stock in its infancy. Just a baby, if you will. Will it grow up to be a successful Super Growth Stock? Will it be only an average stock that chugs along for the rest of its life with minimal gains? Or, worse, will it never become successful at all, only a loser over time? Understanding how a stock matures gives us a new lens through which to view all stocks and reveals a new way to trade them.

As a result, we are able to categorize different stock patterns and test sell rules. One key finding, which has changed the way we think about all stocks, can be summarized in this question: Where is each stock in its lifecycle? Traders talk about the market lifecycle all the time, discussing whether it's the first year of a bull market or the beginning of a downturn. This affects how we think about the market and maybe how heavily invested a trader will become. How often do we ever really consider where a stock is in its lifecycle? Would this also affect how heavily invested we become in a stock? We'll still need to identify high probability stock patterns, but the bottom line comes down to first being able to recognize where any given stock is in its lifecycle.

Knowing where a stock is in its lifecycle, especially if it's early in the game (hence the focus on IPOs), is key in determining how to trade the stock and even how to handle portfolio management. Part of that means recognizing the phases of a Super Growth Stock. After careful study, we found that new issues advance in two phases: *IPO Advance Phase* (IPO-AP) and *Institutional Advance Phase* (I-AP).

IPO Advance Phase (IPO-AP)

The IPO-AP is generally short-lived. This is the initial advance of a new issue. It may or may not create a short IPO or initial base and then rally. Not all IPO-APs begin with an IPO or initial base; some new issues simply move up from Day 1 or within several days. Regardless of how it starts, this advance tends to be of shorter duration, generally fewer than twenty weeks. Our research shows that trading this phase is best handled with short- or intermediate-term sell rules to extract maximum profits. It's possible for the stock in this phase to rally 20 to 100 percent or more.

As quickly as it goes up during this phase, it can come down just as quickly and turn huge profits into big losses if action is not taken. Our research shows that, in most cases, taking profits faster, as with a short-term trade, avoids what likely would be a quick round-trip. If attempting to hold for a longer move, the results often can prove disappointing.

This early action typically is associated with the excitement and publicity surrounding a new equity trading for the first time. It also can be associated with general market action. IPOs can, for example, correct quickly and significantly as the general market stages a downturn. IPOs are subject to analyst downgrades and *secondary offerings* (a post-market sale of shares) that cause the stock to retreat as well.

The IPO-AP can end with a decline of more than 40 percent off the peak of the advance, a decline in price below the entire IPO base structure, or even below the IPO offering price. Some IPOs quickly undercut the IPO-AP, while others never go through the IPO-AP. We call both of these scenarios *IPO Advance Failure* (IPO-AF). Even if a stock exhibits IPO-AF, our research has shown that an IPO that gains 100 percent in a short amount of time early in its lifecycle can turn into a Super Growth Stock later in its life. This is where diligent monitoring is important, in case the stock turns around.

Institutional Due Diligence Phase (I-DDP)

Knowing that a stock that has gone through an IPO-AP is worth watching, a trader might ask "Why would I want to keep my eye on a stock that never had an IPO-AP and has only disappointed by going through IPO-AF?" The answer is that because, at some point, both types of stocks could mature and grow up. If they do, we can find it on the chart by looking for what we call the *Institutional Due Diligence Phase* (I-DDP).

The I-DDP is a separate phase to watch (not trade) that represents a period of consolidation or base-forming process after the completion of the IPO-AP or IPO-AF. Our research has revealed that the I-DDP phase can range from several months to two years or more. This phase in the lifecycle typically wears out or shakes out investors with its long sideways-to-down price action. Toward the end of this phase, perhaps a stock's *liquidity* begins to increase. Maybe the IPO now demonstrates strong fundamentals after initially exhibiting weak earnings and sales. At the time of the IPO, perhaps the general market was also in a downturn, creating resistance and not allowing a particular IPO or any stocks to rise. The stock might have caught the attention of big mutual funds so that the number of funds that own the stock starts to increase.

A stock showing a constructive I-DDP phase should be watched because once the phase is completed, it might form a first *mature base* and *breakout*, confirming that it is under accumulation. This breakout can be treated as a short- to intermediate-term trade. Many stocks during the end of the I-DDP phase start their advance and then stall near a prior high area (on the left side of the consolidation from several months earlier), creating resistance and a temporary ceiling on the stock chart. We call this the *turbulence zone.*

Since it is likely a stock will experience this turbulence and correct at this point, a short- to intermediate-term trade is best. Perhaps investors who initially bought the stock are finally happy that the stock has risen back to where it was purchased; therefore, this turbulence zone forms as original investors bail. The stock may fall back into a basing pattern when approaching a price close to the turbulence zone. If the stock clears the turbulence zone easily and with great strength, it is starting an advance. This is the end of the I-DDP. However, keep in mind that the stock could remain stuck at the turbulence zone or below, never advancing.

Institutional Advance Phase (I-AP)

After the I-DDP is complete, if the stock stages a breakout from a first (or second) mature base and moves beyond the turbulence zone, a long-term hold may be in order. This phase can generate higher profits and typically is the longest-term and least volatile stage of a stock's lifecycle. This is called the Institutional Advance Phase (I-AP). This advance, when successful, tends to be of longer duration; indeed, the study shows an intermediate- to long-term hold trade bias extracts maximum profitability. Generally, this phase occurs only when the new issue is of significant investment quality. It's also the major price advance phase that a trader doesn't want to miss. In this phase, longer-term sell rules are more effective. The general market also might be in an uptrend during this time, which helps propel the stock upward.

The lifecycle phases might take some time to get used to. For easy reference, we have summarized the lifecycle phases in Table 3.1.

Table 3.1 Lifecycle Phases

IPO Advance Phase (1PO-AP)	Institutional Due Diligence Phase (I-DDP)	Institutional Advance Phase (I-AP)
Initial advance of an IPO (typically short-lived).	A long sideways-to-down consolidation process (months to years) after the completion of the IPO Advance Phase or IPO Advance Failure.	Advance out of a mature base after the Institutional Due Diligence Phase (can be the longest stage of the lifecycle).

Prior to making a sustained advance, the majority of Super Growth Stocks go through a long I-DDP. Investors can become worn out or even take the stock off their radar during this phase. We know from our study, though, the exact opposite should be happening. This is a time to be vigilant in monitoring the stock for a breakout. This is one of the golden nuggets of the study: If the potential Super Growth Stock finished its I-DDP phase, staged a breakout from a mature base, and cleared the turbulence zone, then the stock has entered a longer-run phase that is ripe for longer-term sell rules. With that, we'll be glad we never took that stock off our radar.

The final piece of this puzzle is to consider the pattern that develops during these lifecycle phases. Understanding the stock pattern and how it forms in conjunction with the phases creates a one–two combination of how to find big winners early. Let's talk about those lifecycle patterns next.

CHAPTER 4
DISCOVER LIFECYCLE PATTERNS

MANY READERS ALREADY MIGHT BE FAMILIAR with stock patterns of various sorts, such as the Cup and Handle, Flat Base, Ascending Triangle, Parabolic Curve, Wedge Formation, Channel Formation, Symmetrical Triangle, Descending Triangle, Flags and Pennants, Head and Shoulders, and Inverted Heads and Shoulders, just to name a few.[5] As mentioned, as we set out on our study, we watched the chimps and were able to categorize patterns that occur during a growth stock's lifecycle. A chartist might not agree with every pattern as we have identified them. Everyone perceives something different when looking at art. Someone might see a Cup and Handle chart pattern; another trader sees an Inverted Head and Shoulders instead. In the end, we found that it's important to understand both the pattern and the phase for early lifecycle stocks.

Beauty Is in the Eye of the Beholder

When reviewing a stock early in its lifecycle as a possible trade candidate, we first consider the type of pattern it is currently exhibiting. Matching the pattern and knowing the lifecycle phase will help one choose appropriate trading strategies, including sell rules. It's important to note that a lifecycle pattern describes a

---

[5]Source: www.chartpattern.com.

stock's behavior at a given point in time. A stock may resemble one pattern and then morph into another pattern. We are flexible and adapt our choice of rules to the changing patterns.

In this section, we'll share the lifecycle patterns. After each of the six patterns, we'll show a graphic representation along with stocks that fit each category. Later, we'll again refer to these charts as we put all the pieces together.

Late Bloomer Lifecycle Pattern

A *Late Bloomer* has an initial move up from its IPO base. Just as everyone starts to believe it's a leader, this pattern quickly stalls out and wears out investors with a long, sideways move, typically for close to a year or more, before starting a massive rally. In essence, Late Bloomers are those IPOs that initially appear to be great by staging an advance. After a quick advance, though, Late Bloomers quickly fall into IPO-AF (or IPO disease). The initial move is tradeable and part of the IPO-AP we talked about earlier. Once it stalls, the stock goes through the I-DDP before starting the I-AP. Palo Alto Networks is one example of a typical Late Bloomer, see Table 4.1 for additional examples of Late Bloomers.

Table 4.1 Famous Late Bloomers

Symbol	IPO	Symbol	IPO
Chipotle Mexican Grill (CMG)	1-26-2006	Shopify (SHOP)	5-21-2015
Cisco Systems (CSCO)	2-16-1990	Tesla (TSLA)	6-29-2010
Lululemon (LULU)	7-30-2007	Visa (V)	3-19-2008
Palo Alto Networks (PANW)	7-20-2012	Whole Foods (WFM) bought by Amazon	1-23-1992
Qualcomm (QCOM)	12-13-1991	Yelp Inc. (YELP)	3-2-2012

Figures 4.1–4.4 illustrate the Late Bloomer pattern. Note how the stock makes an initial move, stalls out, trades sideways, and then finally makes a longer move. On the Late Bloomer line chart shown in Figure 4.1, note the gray horizontal line. This is the price point at the close of the first trading week for the new issue. This reference point helps to interpret the line chart, specifically the subsequent price action.

For example, in the case of the Late Bloomer, the stock does advance in price initially (as illustrated by the line chart rising above the gray line). Then the stock retraces the initial move and spends a lot of time below the gray line (meaning the price has undercut the initial opening week price action), followed by a regain of the gray line and subsequent rally (which illustrates the start of the I-AP). We have included this reference point (i.e., the gray line) on all the lifecycle pattern line charts for easy reference since they help tell the story of each pattern's unique price path.

In Figure 4.2, we show a block diagram that denotes all the lifecycle phases as well as the potential turbulence zone a stock might experience when reaching a previous price high. In Figure 4.3, we show the Late Bloomer Pattern with the lifecycle phases superimposed on the actual stock chart. Figure 4.4 includes several examples of variations of Late Bloomer patterns. Many traders are looking for the higher-probability trades. Our research has shown that looking for the beginning of the I-AP is a good place to start.

Next, let's refer to the Palo Alto Networks stock chart (Figure 4.3) with the blocks depicting the phases we explained earlier. With practice, a trader can train her eye to quickly spot the phases on a chart.

Late Bloomer

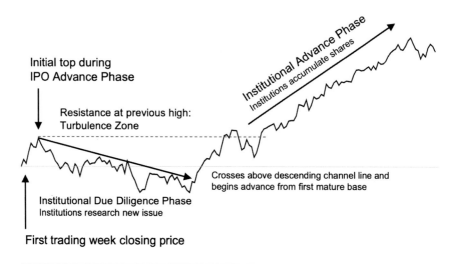

Figure 4.1 Late Bloomer Line Chart

Late Bloomer – Palo Alto Networks (PANW)

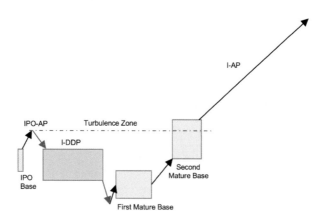

Figure 4.2 Late Bloomer Block Diagram. Lifecycle Phases include: IPO-AP, I-DDP, first mature base, second mature base, I-AP

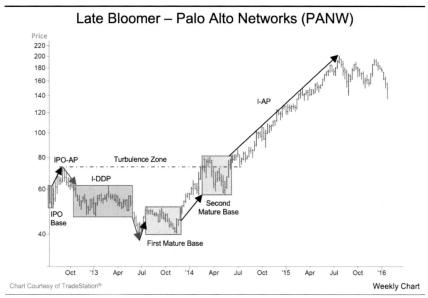

Figure 4.3 Late Bloomer Lifecycle Pattern

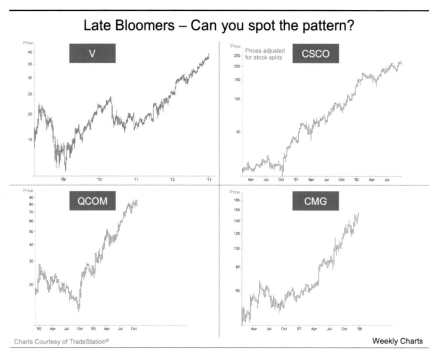

Figure 4.4 The Art of Spotting Late Bloomers

Pump and Dump Lifecycle Pattern

A *Pump and Dump* goes public to much fanfare. This pattern shows, however, that the stock starts to tank soon after the IPO, undercuts its IPO price, and consolidates for several months to a year or more before starting its move up. Many traders get caught in the hype of a new IPO and get trapped in the pump and dump scenario. This can be a dangerous pattern for new investors.

Facebook (FB) is the epitome of Pump and Dump (see Figure 4.7). Just about everyone believed that this stock was going to skyrocket when it launched; instead, it tumbled from Day 1. Note how the line chart in Figure 4.5 stays below the gray line from the initial trading week for more than a year, illustrating the initial failure of the stock. Without a doubt, Facebook was a clear IPO-AF. It took more than a year before Facebook came back to life. Disciplined and patient investors who waited for the right time to buy witnessed a 30 percent upside gap breakout in July 2013, that led to a five-fold move in five years. After a long I-DDP, Facebook was ready for the I-AP and some superior long-term gains, likely due to user growth and positive earnings. Figures 4.5–4.8 illustrate the Pump and Dump pattern along with actual examples.

Table 4.2 Famous Pump and Dumps

Symbol	IPO	Symbol	IPO
Amgen (AMGN)	6-17-1983	Las Vegas Sands (LVS)	12-15-2004
Apple (AAPL)	12-12-1980	LinkedIn (LNKD) bought by Microsoft	5-19-2011
Baidu (BIDU)	8-5-2005	Netflix (NFLX)	5-23-2002
Cboe Global Markets (CBOE)	6-15-2010	Yahoo (YHOO) bought by Verizon	4-12-1996
Facebook (FB)	5-18-2012	Zillow (ZG)	7-20-2011

Pump and Dump

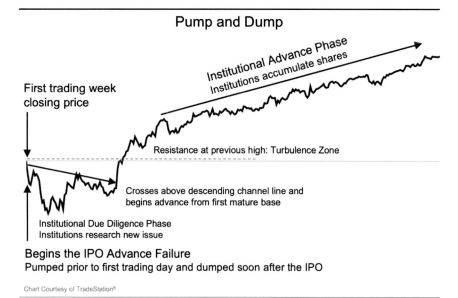

First trading week
closing price

Institutional Advance Phase
Institutions accumulate shares

Resistance at previous high: Turbulence Zone

Crosses above descending channel line and
begins advance from first mature base

Institutional Due Diligence Phase
Institutions research new issue

Begins the IPO Advance Failure
Pumped prior to first trading day and dumped soon after the IPO

Chart Courtesy of TradeStation®

Figure 4.5 Pump and Dump Line Chart

Pump and Dump – Facebook (FB)

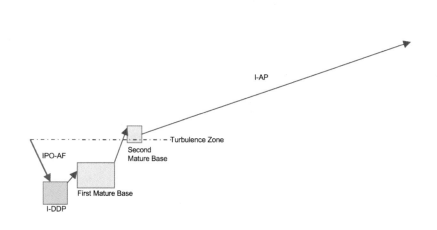

I-AP

Turbulence Zone

IPO-AF

Second
Mature Base

First Mature Base

I-DDP

Figure 4.6 Pump and Dump Block Diagram.
Lifecycle Phases include: IPO-AF, I-DDP, first mature base,
second mature base, I-AP

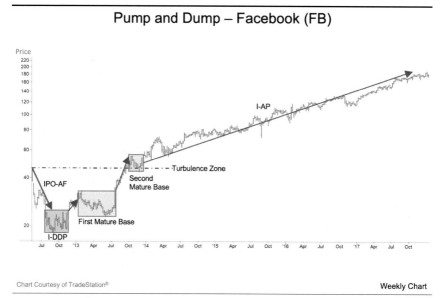

Figure 4.7 Pump and Dump Lifecycle Pattern

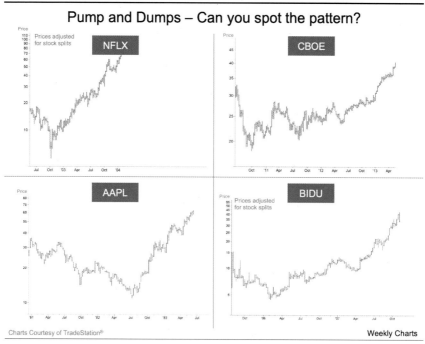

Figure 4.8 The Art of Spotting Pump and Dumps

Stair Stepper Lifecycle Pattern

A *Stair Stepper* typically has at least a 20 percent move up from the IPO base and goes on to form multiple bases (without undercutting the previous base), providing many opportunities to buy along the way up and making it easier to hold through corrections. A Stair Stepper can be one of the best options for those who prefer lower volatility. The pattern usually allows a trader to garner a nice percentage price move from the buy point or *cushion*, and then the stock stair-steps its way to more gains.

Google (Alphabet) is a great example of a Stair Stepper, and a unique example of a stock that did not go through an I-DDP phase. Stair Steppers breakout from an IPO base (or mature base), as shown in Figure 4.11, and immediately start the I-AP. Note on the line chart in Figure 4.9 how the price action undercuts the gray line only briefly and then rises above it, meaning the stock undercut its first weekly close only for a short time and then proceeds directly to an I-AP. Figures 4.9–4.12 illustrate the Stair Stepper pattern along with actual examples.

Table 4.3 Famous Stair Steppers

Symbol	IPO	Symbol	IPO
Alphabet/ Google (GOOGL)	8-19-2004	Mastercard (MA)	5-25-2006
Amazon (AMZN)	5-15-1997	Microsoft (MSFT)	3-13-1986
America Online AOL (TWX) merged with Time Warner	3-19-1992	Nvidia (NVDA)	1-22-1999
CME Group (CME)	12-6-2002	ServiceNow (NOW)	6-29-2012
Juniper Networks (JNPR)	6-25-1999	Starbucks (SBUX)	6-26-1992

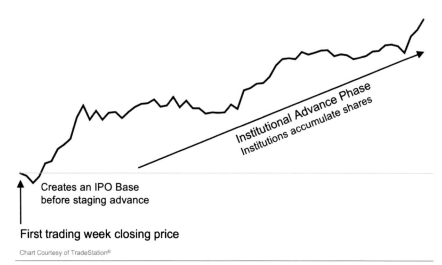

Chart Courtesy of TradeStation®

Figure 4.9 Stair Stepper Line Chart

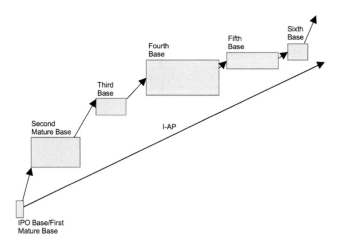

Figure 4.10 Stair Stepper Block Diagram.
Lifecycle Phases include: IPO base moves directly
to I-AP; skips the I-DDP

Figure 4.11 Stair Stepper Lifecycle Pattern

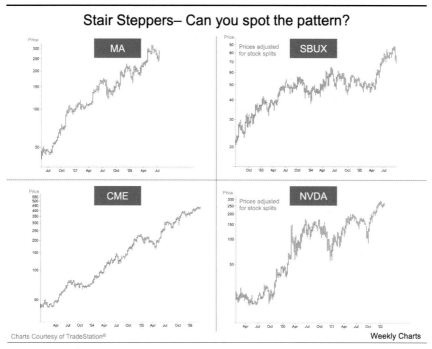

Figure 4.12 The Art of Spotting Stair Steppers

Rocket Ship Lifecycle Pattern

A *Rocket Ship* starts a massive rise immediately—like lifting off a launching pad—from its IPO base, never undercuts its IPO base (or initial base), and continues to rise so quickly that it's difficult to establish a position. eBay's meteoric post-IPO base rise is one of the best examples of a Rocket Ship. (It's also the basis for one of the sell rules that we discuss later.)

eBay moved out of a 21-Day IPO base on a gap move of 46 percent on October 26, 1998. The deep correction (of 50 percent) in the IPO base before the breakout was unusual and likely due to the market environment (a bear market at the time). After the breakout, eBay proceeded to more than triple in ten weeks, as shown in Figure 4.15. After forming an intermediate peak in January 1999 and subsequent top in March 2000 (along with the market), eBay languished for four years before resuming its advance. Figures 4.13–4.16 illustrate the Rocket Ship pattern along with actual examples.

Table 4.4 Famous Rocket Ships

Symbol	IPO	Symbol	IPO
Acacia Communications (ACIA)	5-13-2016	First Solar (FSLR)	11-17-2006
Adobe Systems (ADBE)	8-14-1986	Home Depot (HD)	9-22-1981
Akamai Technologies (AKAM)	10-29-1999	Intercontinental Exchange (ICE)	11-16-2005
eBay (EBAY)	9-24-1998	Michael Kors (KORS)	12-15-2011
FireEye (FEYE)	9-20-2013	VMware (VMW)	8-14-2007

Rocket Ship

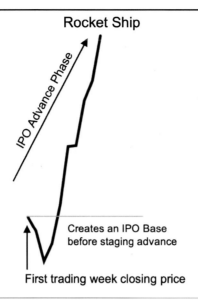

Creates an IPO Base
before staging advance

First trading week closing price

Chart Courtesy of TradeStation®

Figure 4.13 Rocket Ship Line Chart

Rocket Ship – eBay (EBAY)

IPO-AP

IPO Base

Figure 4.14 Rocket Ship Block Diagram.
Lifecycle Phases include: IPO-AP (>100 to 500 percent or more)

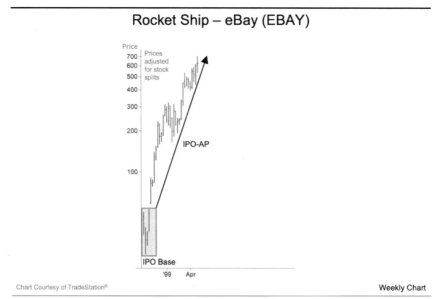

Chart Courtesy of TradeStation®   Weekly Chart

Figure 4.15 Rocket Ship Lifecycle Pattern

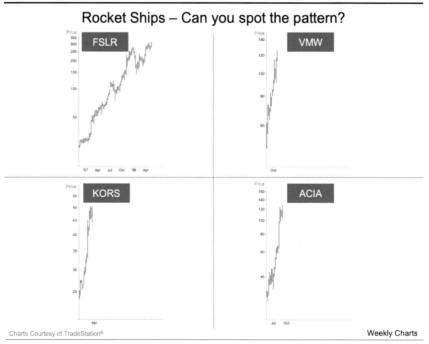

Charts Courtesy of TradeStation®   Weekly Charts

Figure 4.16 The Art of Spotting Rocket Ships

One-Hit Wonder Lifecycle Pattern

An IPO that explodes with big gains, fizzles out, and undercuts the entire structure is a *One-Hit Wonder*. If a trader is fast, and has great *offensive sell rules* or *trailing stops*, he might be able to book some considerable gains before the stock fizzles out.

Shake Shack is a great example of this type of stock. Take a look at Figure 4.17 showing the line chart of Shake Shack's price action. Notice the upside-down, v-shaped move. This is the signature of a One-Hit Wonder. After going public, Shake Shack moved out of a 7-Week initial base and proceeded to almost double in eight weeks; however, it quickly round-tripped the entire IPO-AP and then some, ultimately undercutting the entire structure. Shake Shack then took three years off for its I-DDP before staging a breakout from its first mature base. Maybe it will come back all the way and go on to become a leading stock; however, at the time of this writing, it has yet to do so (although it has completed the I-DDP and started its I-AP).

Keep One-Hit Wonders on a watchlist to monitor if the stocks can complete the I-DDP and form a first mature base breakout. We call these stocks *One-Hit Wonders Plus*, or stocks that come back to lead again. Figures 4.17–4.20 illustrate the One-Hit Wonder pattern along with some examples of both One-Hit Wonders and One-Hit Wonders Plus.

Table 4.5 Famous One-Hit Wonders

Symbol	IPO	Symbol	IPO
Alibaba (BABA) One-Hit Wonder Plus	9-19-2014	Mobileye (MBLY) purchased by Intel	8-1-2014
Autohome (ATHM) One-Hit Wonder Plus	12-11-2013	Shake Shack (SHAK) One-Hit Wonder Plus	1-30-2015
El Pollo Loco (LOCO)	7-25-2014	Twilio (TWLO) One-Hit Wonder Plus	6-23-2016
Fitbit (FIT)	6-18-2015	Twitter (TWTR) One-Hit Wonder Plus	11-7-2013
GoPro (GPRO)	6-26-2014	Zynga (ZNGA)	12-16-2011

One-Hit Wonder

Initial top during IPO Advance Phase

IPO Advance Failure round-trips IPO Advance

First trading week closing price

Institutional Due Diligence Phase
Institutions research new issue

Chart Courtesy of TradeStation®

Figure 4.17 One-Hit Wonder Line Chart

One-Hit Wonder – Shake Shack (SHAK)

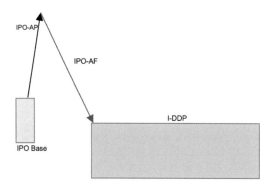

Figure 4.18 One-Hit Wonder Block Diagram.
Lifecycle Phases include: IPO-AP, IPO-AF, I-DDP

One-Hit Wonder – Shake Shack (SHAK)

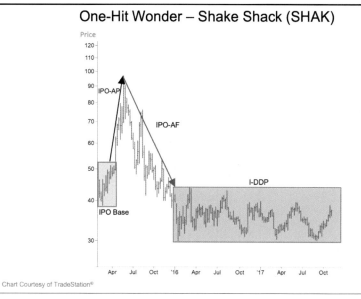

Chart Courtesy of TradeStation®   Weekly Chart

Figure 4.19 One-Hit Wonder Lifecycle Pattern

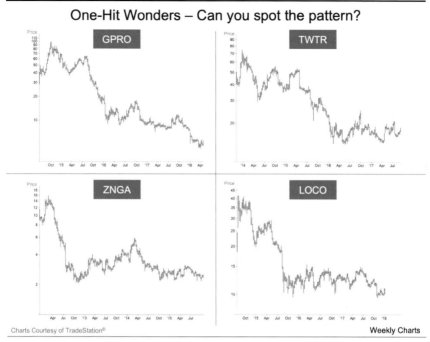

Figure 4.20 The Art of Spotting One-Hit Wonders

Disappointment Lifecycle Pattern

A *Disappointment* represents an IPO that almost immediately starts to tank, undercuts its IPO price, and rarely becomes a leader or, if it does, takes many years to surpass its IPO price. Not all stocks complete the I-DDP and move to I-AP. That's not to say that Disappointments never become leaders. Indeed, as of this writing, Etsy (originally classified as a Disappointment) has completed the I-DDP, staged a mature base breakout, and is in the I-AP near all-time highs in price. Sometimes a company such as Etsy can reinvent itself; when that happens, the stock can snap out of its downtrend and become a leader.

Etsy is an example of a rare turnaround in a Disappointment pattern. For another example, if Facebook had never executed on its mobile strategy, the company might have ended up as a Disappointment rather than a Pump and Dump pattern Super Growth Stock. In this sense, just as with all technical analysis, patterns can morph over time. That's why it's important to even keep Disappointments on a watchlist if they appear to be completing an I-DDP.

Potbelly's stock is another good example of a Disappointment. Some team members thought the stock had potential because stores were crowded and customers seemed to like the reasonably priced sandwiches. Potbelly, at the time of this writing, is in the I-DDP.

This is why it's important to distinguish a good company from a good stock. A good company is not necessarily a good stock. Most never really become the great leader we're always looking for. This was a huge revelation to the team and reinforces the fact that a trader must be highly selective in stock picking, because the great leading stocks of our time are few and far between. Refer to Figures 4.21–4.24 for additional examples and charts of Disappointments.

Table 4.6 Famous Disappointments

Symbol	IPO	Symbol	IPO
Ally Financial (ALLY)	4-10-2014	Lending Club (LC)	12-11-2014
Etsy Inc. (ETSY) completed I-DDP and moved into I-AP	4-16-2015	Noodles & Company (NDLS)	6-28-2013
Extended Stay America (STAY)	11-13-2013	Peak Resorts (SKIS)	11-21-2014
Habit Restaurants (HABT)	11-20-2014	Snap Inc. (SNAP)	3-2-2017

Disappointment

First trading week closing price

IPO Advance Failure

Institutional Due Diligence Phase
Institutions research new issue

Chart Courtesy of TradeStation®

Figure 4.21 Disappointment Line Chart

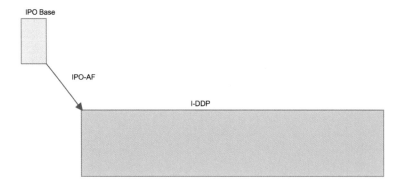

Disappointment – Potbelly (PBPB)

IPO Base

IPO-AF

I-DDP

Figure 4.22 Disappointment Block Diagram.
Lifecycle Phases include: IPO-AF, I-DDP

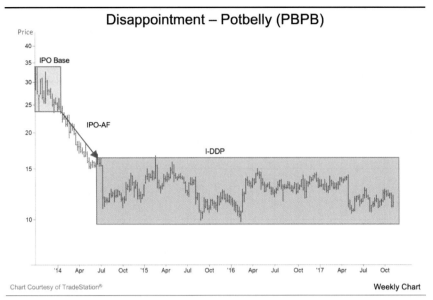

Figure 4.23 Disappointment Lifecycle Pattern

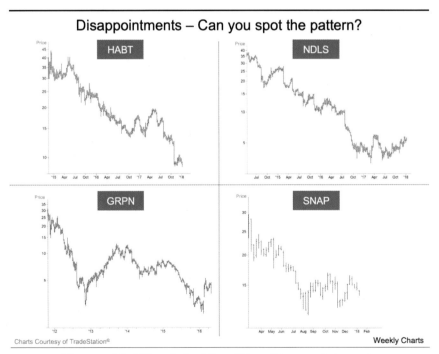

Figure 4.24 The Art of Spotting Disappointments

The patterns we have identified and illustrated in this chapter (see Figure 4.25) highlight some of the key findings of our study; however, remember that patterns are not always easy to interpret. As we have said, chart reading is an art. Some of our team members, for example, read a few charts and determined that a particular stock was a Late Bloomer while others thought it was a Stair Stepper. Such disagreements and discrepancies are to be expected, just as with any other technical analysis of chart patterns. Regardless, these tools aid the avid stock chart reader in identifying those stocks that might be Super Growth Stocks.

Armed with this new methodology, let's review how lifecycle phases and patterns play out with the trading rules we have tested. It's time to see where the potential profits from these Super Growth Stocks will land.

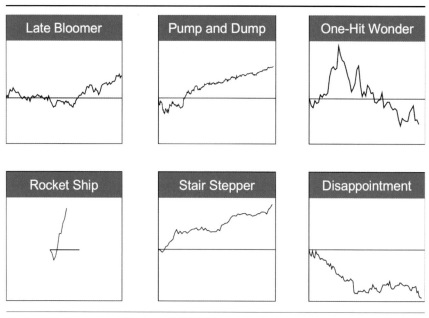

Figure 4.25 Lifecycle Patterns

CHAPTER 5
LIFECYCLE TRADING RULES

EMOTIONS CAN GET IN THE WAY of sound trading—even though we shouldn't let them. Despite our best efforts, most of us let our emotions get the best of us from time to time. Trading volatile stocks, for example, might well cause some sleepless nights and emotional trading. We can limit reckless trading by relying on well-tested sell rules to guide us.

Of course, every trader is different—even those of us on our research team. So it's important to pick the rules that work best for each trader's unique style, timeframe, and ability to withstand drawdowns. Our research has revealed some effective buy and sell rules, which we'll examine next.

Super Growth Stock Buy Rules

Knowing when to buy is one of the hardest lessons to learn. Most of us have been burned many times, especially as novice investors, because we've missed the buy point and bought extended (3 to 10 percent or more above the proper breakout buy point), only to take a significant loss later. This can lead to painful losses because, as soon as the stock retreats in price, the hit can be much larger than if the stock had been bought just as it cleared a consolidation.

So, what is a proper buy point? In this study, we defined the buy points used in order to have a level playing field for all the results. For the study, our approach focused on buy points out of consolidations or bases. There is an art to reading a stock chart, and we found that the buy point can differ even using this buy point approach. However, the variations were somewhat minimal, and at the end of the day, we hand-selected and agreed to four buy points where the stock broke into a new high after:

1. IPO base: a short consolidation within seven weeks of the IPO start date; or
2. Consolidation or initial base: a base greater than seven weeks from IPO start date (prior to I-DDP); or
3. *Breakaway gap*: a significantly higher opening and closing price (often 25 percent or more) from the prior day's close on increased volume from an IPO base, initial base, or first mature base; or
4. First mature base: a base that forms after the I-DDP.

Although buy points can be specific to a trading style, the above buy points we used in the study are typical for growth stock trend traders. While some traders like to buy low, we are growth stock trend investors (primarily long positions), and we never try to catch a falling knife (i.e., buy a stock that is in a downtrend) on the hope that it has bottomed. We like to buy breakouts (i.e., when a stock clears resistance) and sell higher. That's always the goal.

Lifecycle Sell Rules

Sell rules are often specific to each trader's timeframe and trading style. Everyone has a different trading style, and each one of us on the team has a different trading style as well. In the *lifecycle sell rules* we describe below, we each have our own favorites for one reason or another. This begged the question: Which sell rules are most profitable?

Our team's goal was to identify the best sell rules for Super Growth Stocks based on profits, drawdowns, and time-in-market. With that, we had to think about what rules we already knew, which rules we actually use, and, ultimately, which rules would be best for each phase and pattern in a stock's lifecycle for IPOs and Super Growth Stocks. We determined that we would use these rules on each pattern we identified to see how they performed within this framework by simulating each trade with an initial $100,000 investment. Regardless of the sell rule, we had a 10 percent *stop-loss rule* for all trades. We used TradeStation programming to automate the testing process. While we tested many rules, listed below are the four best-performing rules: Ascender, Midterm, 40-Week, and Everest.[6] Following the specifics of each sell rule, we answered these questions:

1. How was the rule developed? What problem does the rule try to solve?

2. What lifecycle phase and pattern is best for this rule?

3. In practice, what are the strengths and weaknesses of this sell rule?

4. What was the performance of this rule for our selected Super Growth Stocks in terms of median percent gain and drawdown in dollars from the peak price during the holding period based on the simulated $100,000 investment?[7]

---

[6]Ascender Rule authored by Eve Boboch; 40-Week Rule authored by Kathy Donnelly; Everest Rule authored by Eric Krull. The Midterm Rule is based on an unpublished sequence of rules originally developed by founder and CIO of Single A Capital, Ajay Jani, and used with permission for this study.

[7]Drawdowns are calculated from the peak price to the lowest price during the holding period.

Ascender Rule

The *Ascender Rule* is designed to capture a quick, powerful move in a stock that has recently gone public and is showing tremendous positive momentum. In other words, the rule is used to capture the majority of profits during the IPO-AP. Using this rule, a portion of the position is held in case the stock continues to advance directly to the I-AP. We consider this an offensive sell rule with a defensive component. The criteria for the rule are as follows:

- Sell 1/2 on daily close at 3 percent below 21-Day EMA.[8]
- Sell 1/4 on daily close at 3 percent below 50-Day SMA.
- Sell last 1/4 only if it undercuts purchase price or after 18 months from buy point or after +500 percent, whichever comes first.

Study results show that the Ascender Rule performs well during both the IPO-AP and I-AP, and particularly well for stocks exhibiting superior strength as in the Rocket Ship and Stair Stepper pattern.

The strengths of the Ascender Rule include locking in some profits in a big winner early and having potential for much larger profits on a portion of the position that is held longer. Lower drawdowns also make this rule attractive compared to some of the other sell rules tested. The weaknesses of the Ascender Rule include the possibility of selling a position too early or giving back profits on a portion of the position.

The Ascender Rule had a median gain of 51 percent along with a median $57,000 drawdown. The Ascender Rule performed particularly well on eBay's advance, which started in October 1998, soon after its IPO.

---

[8]Unless otherwise specified, the following moving averages were used for testing sell rules in the study: 21-Day Exponential Moving Averages (21-Day EMA) and 50-Day, 10-Week, and 40-Week Simple Moving Averages (SMAs).

Midterm Rule

The *Midterm Rule* is designed to avoid selling a big winner too early and attempts to hold for an I-AP. This rule typically would be applied after the I-DDP at the start of the I-AP, ideally after the turbulence zone. We consider this a *defensive sell rule*. The criteria for the rule are as follows:

- After two closes under the 10-Week SMA, sell at 6 percent (intraday) below the low of those two weeks (intermediate-term trigger); or
- sell on first weekly close below 10-Week SMA after 1-Year hold (long-term trigger); or
- sell if the stock closes the week 30 percent off its peak; or
- sell if the weekly close is below the 40-Week SMA.

Study results show that the Midterm Rule performs better during the I-AP as compared to the IPO-AP due to the fact the I-AP is generally a less volatile phase. In our sample testing, the rule has worked particularly well for Pump and Dump and Stair Stepper patterns.

The main strength of the Midterm Rule is the potential for much larger profits on a big winner since the position typically is held through normal corrections. The main weakness of the Midterm Rule is the large drawdown when the rule triggers a sell signal as compared to most of the other rules.

The Midterm Rule had a median gain of 70 percent along with a median $66,000 drawdown. The Midterm Rule performed particularly well on Facebook's advance, which started with a breakaway gap in July 2013 after the I-DDP was completed.

40-Week Rule

The *40-Week Rule* is designed to hold a big winner for a significant amount of time (over a year or more) during the I-AP in order to achieve large gains. We consider this a defensive sell rule. The criterion for the rule is as follows:

- Sell on first weekly (Friday) close greater than 1 percent below 40-Week SMA.

Study results show that the 40-Week Rule performs well when attempting to hold a big winner after the I-DDP and during the I-AP. In our testing sample, this rule works particularly well for Stair Stepper, Late Bloomer, and Pump and Dump patterns.

The main strength of the 40-Week Rule is the potential for life-changing profits when applied to the right stock, such as Amazon, that trends above the 40-Week SMA. The main weakness of the 40-Week Rule is the very large drawdown as compared to all the other rules we tested.

40-Week Rule had a median gain of 81 percent along with a median $102,000 drawdown. The 40-Week Rule performed particularly well on Amazon's amazing move from its initial base in 1997.

Everest Rule

The *Everest Rule* is designed to attempt to minimize drawdowns while selling into strength and being able to still participate in a portion of the massive moves of big winners. This rule is best used near the end of the I-AP phase and during the IPO-AP. This is a sell rule with an offensive trigger point and a fast, defensive trailing stop. The criterion for the rule is as follows:

- Sell when a stock makes a *parabolic move* and closes below the intraday low from two days earlier. If the stock gapped up the previous day, wait for a close below the low of the gap day as a sell point. This rule resets as the stock makes new highs.

The Everest Rule is designed to work for both the IPO-AP and I-AP, and study results confirmed the efficacy of this. In our testing sample, this rule works particularly well for some One-Hit Wonders and Rocket Ships.

The main strength of the Everest Rule is the low drawdown as compared to all the other rules we tested. The main weakness of the Everest Rule is selling too early. On rare occasions when a stock makes a parabolic move up over several days, even the Everest Rule can compel you to sell late, causing huge drawdowns off the peak.

The Everest Rule had a median 52 percent gain along with a median $33,000 drawdown. The Everest Rule performed particularly well as a sell rule for Shake Shack's advance as we'll see later.

Although we used high-performance stocks in our study, we found that these lifecycle sell rules, along with a stop-loss rule as mentioned earlier, can help limit losses if the stock performs poorly. This underperformance could be due to stock specific issues or because the general market could be due for a correction, dragging most stocks down with it.

The study team sets stop-losses at no more than 1 percent of capital per trade (as a maximum). As a trader gains more experience, it's possible to significantly tighten stop-loss points. We used a stop-loss of 10 percent (from the buy point) in our study due to the volatility of early lifecycle stocks (larger than what we use for mature stocks). Even so, we are prepared to possibly be *stopped-out* several times before getting positioned at the right time. If a trader discovers a Super Growth Stock early in its lifecycle, these sell rules can help assist in holding for larger profits through the inevitable corrections.

Although we have shared a preview of some of the performance results of each of the rules above, in the next section, we provide the detailed performance numbers of the sell rules and the actual results that would have been incurred had they been used on our *iconic stock* examples.

Sell Rules Performance

Choosing an appropriate rule for a specific trade should focus on parameters such as lifecycle phase and pattern, ability to withstand profit drawdowns, and trading personality. As noted in the definitions of each rule, we highlighted which worked best based on our study results. As we will show in the iconic examples later in this chapter, during the advance, there are periods of huge drawdowns. Many traders might not be able to stomach that kind of action. The goal, of course, is to avoid cutting profits short while at the same time avoiding as much of the painful drawdowns that so many traders have trouble managing.

Tables 5.1 and 5.2 summarize test results for how the lifecycle sell rules performed on a sample of Super Growth Stocks. The tables illustrate how the rules performed, including median percent gain and median dollar drawdown by lifecycle pattern for a simulated $100,000 investment.

For example, the 40-Week Rule produces the largest median profits of 81 percent; however, the 40-Week Rule has large median profit drawdowns of $102,000 as shown in Table 5.2. The Midterm Rule produces median profits of 70 percent, higher than the Ascender Rule profits of 51 percent; however, the Ascender Rule has lower median drawdowns of $57,000 versus $66,000.

Of the four rules tested, the Everest Rule had the most impressive, lowest median profit drawdown of $33,000 (see Table 5.2). We determined that the Everest Rule can be used to minimize drawdowns; however, the tradeoff is that the rule sells much too early. For example, this was the case for eBay and Amazon.

Which sell rules work best under which circumstances can be determined by the lifecycle phase (IPO-AP or I-AP), lifecycle pattern, and type of stock being traded. Figure 5.1 illustrates these rules.

Table 5.1 Sell Rules Performance by Category

Sell Rules	Late Bloomer		One-Hit Wonder		Pump and Dump		Rocket Ship		Stair Stepper	
	Median % Gain	Median Drawdown (Dd) $K	Median % Gain	Median Dd $K	Median % Gain	Median Dd $K	Median % Gain	Median Dd $K	Median % Gain	Median Dd $K
Ascender	11%	$49	5%	$46	86%	$54	91%	$76	198%	$65
Midterm	66%	$62	4%	$60	97%	$51	43%	$69	167%	$94
40-Week	69%	$69	-10%	$53	106%	$136	109%	$102	272%	$238
Everest	26%	$33	20%	$35	64%	$41	53%	$32	60%	$25

Table 5.2 Sell Rules Performance Summary

Sell Rules	Results Across All Stock Categories			
	Median % Gain	Median Drawdown $K	Median % of Peak Profit Retained	Median Time in Market (Days)
Ascender	51%	$57	48%	503
Midterm	70%	$66	45%	201
40-Week	81%	$102	41%	374
Everest	52%	$33	63%	87

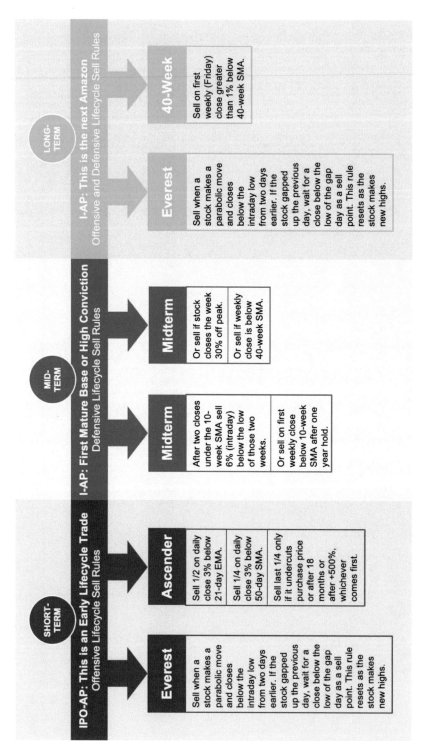

Figure 5.1 Lifecycle Sell Rules

Now that we have explained the phases of a stock's lifecycle, the patterns we found, and the rules we used to test what we learned, it's time to look at several iconic stocks—which are among some of the best historical examples of Super Growth Stocks. We have included the sell points for all the lifecycle sell rules—Everest, Ascender, 40-Week, and Midterm—on all the charts in this chapter.

Iconic Super Growth Stocks

We mentioned several big winners in the introduction of this book, among them Amazon, Tesla, Netflix, and Google. Let's look at how the lifecycle sell rules performed on all the stocks we have discussed.

In the figures below, we identify for each iconic stock the buy and sell points for each rule as well as percent gain, drawdown, *percent of peak profit retained*, and length of hold. The examples to follow can help provide a sense of what a trader would have to withstand to profit.

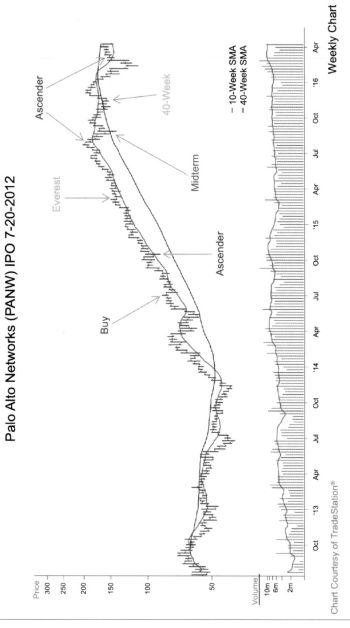

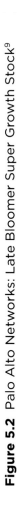

Figure 5.2 Palo Alto Networks: Late Bloomer Super Growth Stock[9]

[9]For all charts in this book, we developed modified moving average lines to help us analyze how a stock is performing early after its IPO. We use rolling averages until the maximum amount of time has passed for that specific moving average. For example, the 10-Week SMA is calculated as follows: there is no moving average line for Week 1, but for Week 2, it is calculated by taking the average weekly closing price for the first two weeks. For Week 3, it is the average weekly closing prices for the first

Our first example comes from Palo Alto Networks (PANW), which is a Late Bloomer (see Figure 5.2).

The buy point shown for Palo Alto Networks was the first mature base breakout as the stock started its I-AP after a 2-Year I-DDP. Since Palo Alto Networks moved sideways for years, consolidating before starting the I-AP (with just a short-lived IPO-AP), it is considered a Late Bloomer. With a simulated $100,000 investment, our findings revealed that the most profitable sell rule for *iconic Super Growth Stock* Palo Alto Networks was the 40-Week Rule, which generated more than $77,000 in profits. Table 5.3 shows returns for the other rules as well. Applying the 40-Week Rule to PANW would have required some conviction, as evident from the $68,000 drawdown. For those without that kind of wherewithal, the Everest Rule with the lowest drawdown also would have been a winning choice, with a profit of $60,000. The I-AP was strong and steady on this stock in that it held the 10-Week SMA for the majority of its advance.

Table 5.3 Sell Rule Results for Super Growth Stock Palo Alto Networks ($100K Investment)

Sell Rules	Percent Gain	Drawdown $K	Percent of Peak Profit Retained	Days in Market	Sell Rule Trigger
Ascender	59%	$59	50%	545	18-Month Hold
Midterm	66%	$62	52%	354	Intermediate-Term
40-Week	78%	$68	53%	440	Close Below 40-Week SMA
Everest	60%	$22	74%	188	Everest Trailing Stop

three weeks, and continues until finally ten weeks have elapsed. Similarly, the 40-Week SMA is calculated in the same way until forty weeks have elapsed. Lastly, the fuchsia colored SMA volume line shown on the bottom of the chart is also a modified moving average line and is calculated in the same way as the moving averages using the average volume until ten weeks have elapsed and a true 10-Week Volume SMA is achieved.

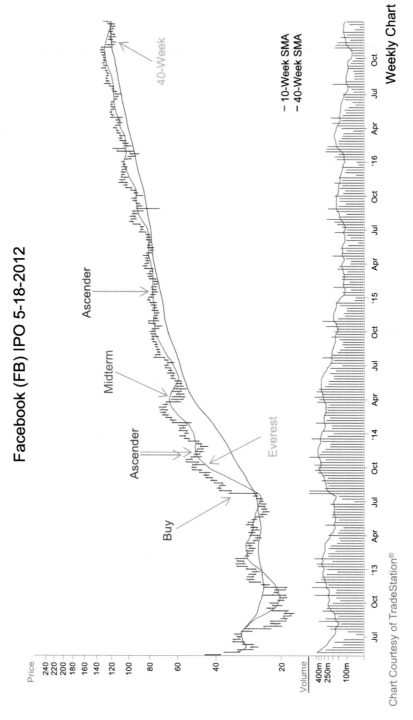

Figure 5.3 Facebook: Pump and Dump Super Growth Stock

Our second example comes from Facebook (FB), which had an initial Pump and Dump pattern (see Figure 5.3). As demonstrated earlier, notice how Facebook immediately starts to fall after its first trading day and takes more than a year of sideways-to-down action before it forms its first mature base. This type of immediate sell-off after going public is the signature of a Pump and Dump pattern.

The buy point shown for Facebook was the first mature base breakaway gap breakout as the stock started its I-AP after a 14-Month I-DDP. Our findings revealed that the most profitable sell rule for Facebook was the 40-Week Rule, with a gain of 250 percent, more than double the next best sell rule, which was the Midterm Rule. After a long I-DDP, the I-AP emerged. Table 5.4 shows returns for the other rules as well.

Table 5.4 Sell Rule Results for Super Growth Stock Facebook ($100K Investment)

Sell Rules	Percent Gain	Drawdown $K	Percent of Peak Profit Retained	Days in Market	Sell Rule Trigger
Ascender	83%	$28	75%	546	18-Month Hold
Midterm	117%	$53	69%	443	Long-Term
40-Week	250%	$81	76%	1,215	Close Below 40-Week SMA
Everest	40%	$13	75%	76	Everest Trailing Stop

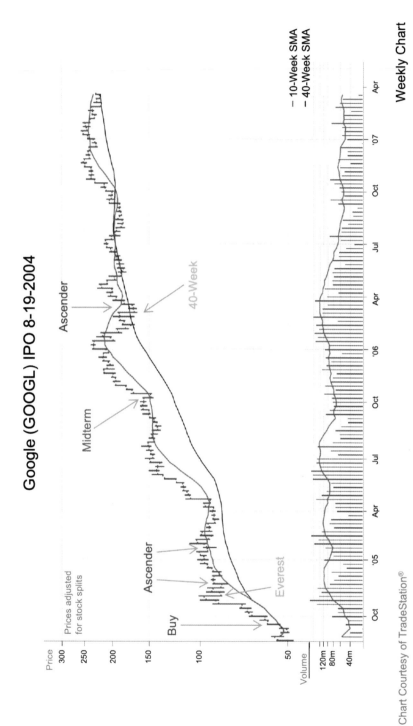

Figure 5.4 Google: Stair Stepper Super Growth Stock

Our next example, Google, falls into the Stair Stepper pattern (see Figure 5.4). As demonstrated earlier, notice how Google never undercuts its IPO base breakout, continues to form bases, and stages breakouts over and over again (without undercutting the previous base). Google staged an I-AP phase right from the start.

The buy point shown for Google was the IPO base breakout as the stock immediately started its I-AP just four weeks after its public debut. It's important to note that this iconic stock bypassed the IPO-AP and I-DDP and went directly to the I-AP. In this example, it's clear that Google, a Stair Stepper Super Growth Stock, was most profitable when the 40-Week Rule was applied. The Midterm Rule also performed well with a strong gain, lower drawdown, and less time in market. If a trader had held through a fairly sizeable drawdown—more than three times the next best option—profits would have come in about 40 percent better using the 40-Week Rule, as shown in Table 5.5.

Table 5.5 Sell Rule Results for Super Growth Stock Google ($100K Investment)

Sell Rules	Percent Gain	Drawdown $K	Percent of Peak Profit Retained	Days in Market	Sell Rule Trigger
Ascender	131%	$63	67%	546	18-Month Hold
Midterm	162%	$39	81%	395	Long-Term
40-Week	200%	$126	61%	544	Close Below 40-Week SMA
Everest	60%	$17	78%	51	Everest Trailing Stop

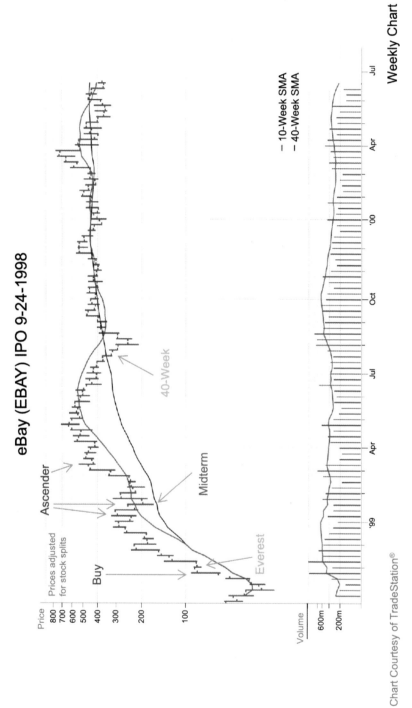

Figure 5.5 eBay: Rocket Ship Super Growth Stock

The next example is of Rocket Ship Super Growth Stock eBay (see Figure 5.5). As demonstrated earlier, notice how eBay forms an IPO base and makes a powerful, near-vertical thrust for several months before taking a breather to consolidate. This type of powerful IPO-AP rally is the signature of the rare Rocket Ship pattern.

The buy point shown for eBay was the IPO base breakaway gap breakout as the stock started its IPO-AP just four weeks after its public debut. As mentioned, eBay's IPO base was unusually deep (more than 50 percent), although it occurred during a bear market. Here we see that eBay was most profitable when the Ascender Rule was applied (see Table 5.6). Note that gains were best here among the sell rules, although the drawdown was second worst. In general, the Ascender Rule performs well on Rocket Ship patterns.

Table 5.6 Sell Rule Results for Super Growth Stock eBay ($100K Investment)

Sell Rules	Percent Gain	Drawdown $K	Percent of Peak Profit Retained	Days in Market	Sell Rule Trigger
Ascender	401%	$194	67%	133	500% Gain
Midterm	274%	$164	63%	82	30% Off Peak
40-Week	381%	$581	40%	273	Close Below 40-Week SMA
Everest	22%	$22	51%	10	Everest Trailing Stop

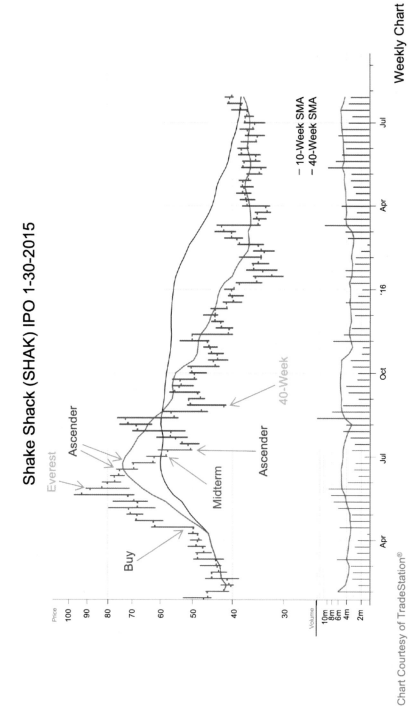

Figure 5.6 Shake Shack: One-Hit Wonder Super Growth Stock

In our last example, One-Hit Wonder Shake Shack (see Figure 5.6) forms a consolidation and has a strong IPO-AP before correcting significantly and undercutting its first base. At the time of this writing, it appears to have completed its I-DDP, staged a breakout from its first mature base, and is moving into an I-AP. This example underscores the importance of continuing to monitor One-Hit Wonders during the I-DDP even after undercutting the entire IPO-AP rally and IPO base structure since they can turn into One-Hit Wonders Plus.

The buy point shown for Shake Shack is the initial base breakout as the stock started its IPO-AP twelve weeks after its public debut. As we can see in Table 5.7, the Everest Rule produced the highest gain while incurring the smallest drawdown. The 40-Week Rule showed a loss which isn't surprising—One-Hit Wonder patterns are usually very quick to reverse after the initial run. The losses were above the 10 percent stop-loss since the automated rules were programmed to sell the next day, and unfortunately, the stock gapped down.

Table 5.7 Sell Rule Results for Super Growth Stock Shake Shack ($100K Investment)

Sell Rules	Percent Gain	Drawdown $K	Percent of Peak Profit Retained	Days in Market	Sell Rule Trigger
Ascender	17%	$73	19%	88	Below Purchase Price
Midterm	21%	$69	23%	75	30% Off Peak
40-Week	-18%	$107	0%	133	Close Below 40-Week SMA
Everest	61%	$35	64%	44	Everest Trailing Stop

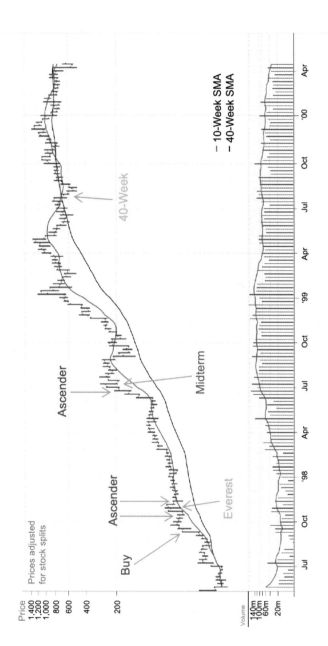

Figure 5.7 Amazon: Stair Stepper Super Growth Stock

We have included the following charts of Super Growth Stocks Amazon, Netflix, and Tesla to illustrate sell rule results for review and further study (see Figures 5.7–5.9 and Tables 5.8–5.10).

Table 5.8 Sell Rule Results for Super Growth Stock Amazon ($100K Investment)

Sell Rules	Percent Gain	Drawdown $K	Percent of Peak Profit Retained	Days in Market	Sell Rule Trigger
Ascender	296%	$53	85%	293	500% Gain
Midterm	523%	$305	63%	309	30% Off Peak[10]
40-Week	1,805%	$2,547	41%	696	Close Below 40-Week SMA
Everest	52%	$50	51%	53	Everest Trailing Stop

---

[10]For the study, we modified the Midterm Rule to require the stock to close the week at 30 percent below the peak price, versus selling on an intraday move as the rule was originally written. For Amazon, this did not occur until November 14, 1997.

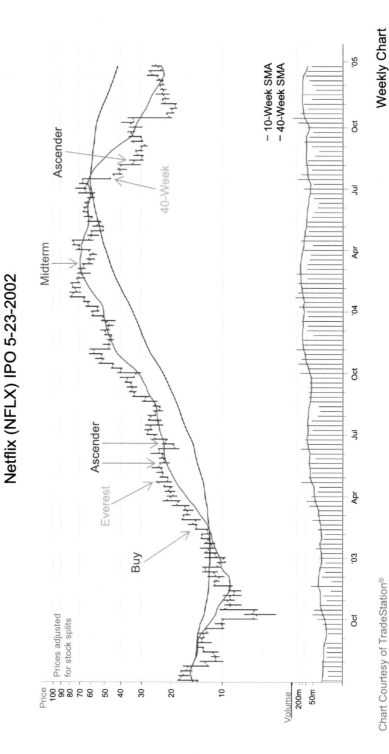

Figure 5.8 Netflix: Pump and Dump Super Growth Stock

Table 5.9 Sell Rule Results for Super Growth Stock Netflix ($100K Investment)

Sell Rules	Percent Gain	Drawdown $K	Percent of Peak Profit Retained	Days in Market	Sell Rule Trigger
Ascender	89%	$182	33%	546	18-Month Hold
Midterm	391%	$141	73%	386	Long-Term
40-Week	225%	$265	46%	521	Close Below 40-Week SMA
Everest	52%	$34	60%	69	Everest Trailing Stop

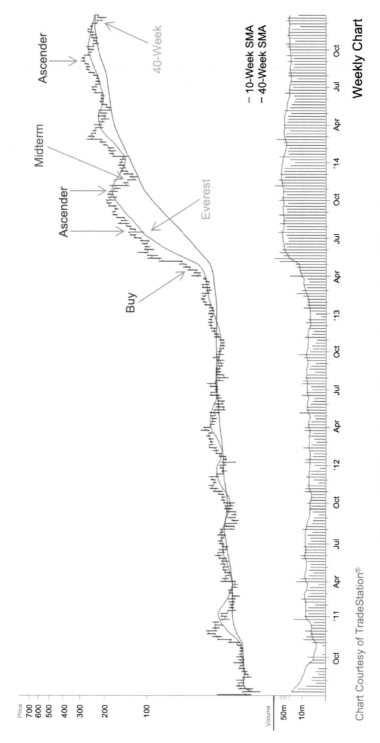

Figure 5.9 Tesla: Late Bloomer Super Growth Stock

Table 5.10 Sell Rule Results for Super Growth Stock
Tesla ($100K Investment)

Sell Rules	Percent Gain	Drawdown $K	Percent of Peak Profit Retained	Days in Market	Sell Rule Trigger
Ascender	353%	$100	78%	503	500% Gain
Midterm	202%	$133	60%	205	Intermediate-Term
40-Week	375%	$188	67%	599	Close Below 40-Week SMA
Everest	128%	$57	69%	90	Everest Trailing Stop

The charts of these iconic Super Growth Stocks reveal that even when trading these elite performers, a trader needs to expect to experience stop-outs (before getting positioned correctly) and drawdowns (while holding for big moves). Of course, as with all stock trading, and especially when trading volatile growth stocks, money management and stock selection is key. We'll discuss further in later chapters, but first, let's look at some stock data over the past thirty years and discuss why searching for future iconic Super Growth Stocks is worth it.

CHAPTER 6
LEVERAGING THE DATA
FOR SUCCESS

MANY QUESTIONS AROSE after we discovered the lifecycle patterns and phases—questions such as: How many stocks during the past thirty years performed well after their IPO? How many were failures? How fast did the stocks move? Should we buy stocks soon after their IPO debut?

The only way to answer these and other questions was to study as many stocks as possible. Otherwise, we would have developed conclusions that would have been insufficient at best, and, worse, could have been misleading or might have caused us to make wrong decisions.

Once again, we used TradeStation to help us accomplish the task. We were able to analyze 1,679 stocks that went public from January 1, 1982, through May 1, 2017. We built a database that captured key dates and price milestones, which allowed us to find answers to our questions. In this chapter, we will explain what the data say. And we'll answer the main question: Is it worth looking for Super Growth Stocks?

Analyzing the Data
Our first question asks how many stocks performed well after their public debut. To answer that question, we first had to define what it meant for an IPO to perform well. We decided that performance

would best be measured by how much the stocks gained and how quickly they advanced. Our benchmark for gains was doubling or more in price from the first day's closing price, and how long it took. This was important to us because if a large percentage of IPOs doubled in a short amount of time, then the odds would be in our favor. Table 6.1 summarizes our findings.

Table 6.1 IPOs That Achieved 100 Percent Gains

Time from Day 1	% of Stocks That Have Achieved at Least 100% Gain
4 Weeks	1.3%
13 Weeks	6%
52 Weeks	20%
4 Years	40%
10 Years	**51%**

As you can see in Table 6.1, just 6 percent of the 1,679 stocks in our sample posted quick gains from the start and doubled or more within thirteen weeks—i.e., their first quarter of trading. Table 6.1 provides the answer to the question of how quickly one should invest in a stock once it goes through its IPO: There is no need to invest quickly in the vast majority of stocks since a majority or 80 percent of IPOs take more than 52 weeks to increase 100 percent or more. And for that matter, even after 10 years, only 51 percent at least double in price.

To further define why it is important to wait before investing in a recent IPO, we studied the number of stocks that undercut their Day 1 price range. We found that 55 percent of all stocks undercut their Day 1 price range within three weeks, as shown in Figure 6.1. This points to the desirability of waiting for a recent IPO to undercut its Day 1 low and form an IPO base prior to considering a buy point. The figure also shows that 91 percent of all stocks eventually undercut their Day 1 price range. Given most stocks will revisit their Day 1 price or fall lower within three weeks of their IPO, the research shows there is no need to jump in and succumb to the Day 1 excitement surrounding a hot stock debut.

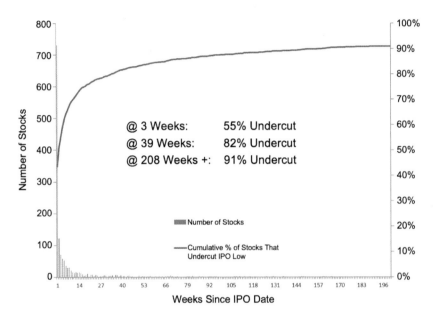

Figure 6.1 Time to Undercut IPO Day 1 Price Low

Another way to study whether we should buy IPOs right away was to investigate how many stocks would trigger our 10 percent stop-loss sell rule. Assuming a trader would buy a stock on the first day it traded, at the lowest price of Day 1, we analyzed how many stocks undercut their Day 1 low price by 10 percent. It's rare that a buyer gets the best price of the day, but we wanted to see the best results that could be achieved by giving the trader as much room as possible to stay in the stock. Figure 6.2 shows the results.

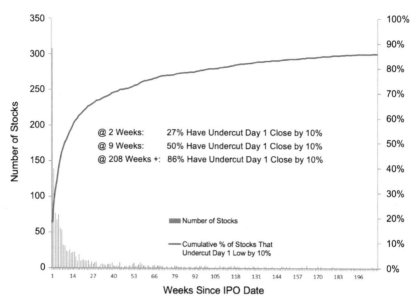

Figure 6.2 Time to Undercut IPO Day 1 Price Low by 10 Percent

The horizontal axis in Figure 6.2 shows the time in weeks after the IPO date. The blue vertical bars show the number of stocks (shown on the left vertical axis) that would trigger a 10 percent stop-loss as measured from their Day 1 IPO low price. Figure 6.2 illustrates that more than three hundred of the stocks studied dropped 10 percent or more within a week after their first day of trading. The red upward sloping line displays the cumulative percent of stocks (as shown on the right vertical scale) that triggered a 10 percent stop-loss within the weeks shown at each point on the horizontal time axis. Approximately 50 percent of all stocks dropped at least 10 percent below their IPO Day 1 low prices within nine weeks. At one hundred four weeks (i.e., two years), more than 80 percent of all stocks had dropped 10 percent or more below their IPO Day 1 low and would have triggered a stop-loss signal. Notice on the far-right hand side of the chart that 86 percent of all stocks would trigger a 10 percent stop-loss. Since 50 percent of IPOs trigger a stop-loss of 10 percent within nine weeks, this is another compelling reason not to invest in a stock right away after it has its IPO.

What about the stocks that are successful and post large gains soon after they start trading? We noticed that many of the stocks that made fast gains of greater than 100 percent tended to correct sharply soon thereafter. We further studied those stocks to determine how quickly they corrected and dropped 50 percent in price. Knowing this information would help us determine if holding through their price corrections is profitable. Our findings are summarized in Table 6.2.

Table 6.2 IPOs Since 1982: Time to Achieve 100 Percent Gains

Of 1,679 IPOs Since 1982	IPO Advance Phase Time to Achieve 100% Gain			
	≤8 Weeks	>8 Weeks but ≤13 Weeks	>13 Weeks but ≤26 Weeks	**Total ≤26 Weeks**
Number of stocks that achieved 100% gain within time frame	55	45	94	194
Percent of stocks that achieved 100% gain within time frame	3.3%	2.7%	5.6%	11.6%
Number of achieving stocks that corrected 50% within next 52 weeks	47	29	63	139
Percent of achieving stocks that corrected 50% within next 52 weeks	86%	64%	67%	72%
Buy-and-Hold Gain Survival Rate	**14%**	**36%**	**33%**	**28%**

Also as shown in Table 6.2, we found fifty-five stocks that doubled or better in price in eight weeks or less from their first trading day close. Of these, 86 percent dropped 50 percent or more in price within the next year. We used a 50 percent drop as a benchmark because it represented a stock that had gained 100 percent and gave back all its gains.

Table 6.2 also shows other timeframes for achieving gains of 100 percent followed by 50 percent corrections. The last column tells the main story: 72 percent of stocks that gained more than 100 percent during their first six months of trading gave back all their gains within the next year. That's almost three of every four stocks, which gives us a strong reason not to try the buy-and-hold strategy at this phase of a stock's lifecycle.

Our research shows that sell rules that lock in shorter-term gains are necessary during the IPO-AP for most stocks. However, we keep on a watchlist those IPOs that make fast gains since our data analysis found that stocks that make fast gains of 100 percent or more in ninety days or less are two times more likely to go on for much higher gains of 500 percent or more.

What About Liquidity?

In addition to studying the price performance of stocks, we wanted to study the volume of shares traded. We needed to know how many stocks traded enough shares per day for us to consider trading them. We used $20 million per day as a benchmark of liquidity. This number is derived by taking the number of shares traded per day times the closing price of the stock. For example, a $20 stock that averages 1 million shares traded per day equals $20 million per day of volume. The reason we chose this number is that many institutional investors won't trade in stocks that have lower liquidity.

A stock needs institutional investors to drive the price higher. Institutional investors such as mutual funds, pension funds, and hedge funds need to acquire a large number of shares in an individual company in order to establish a position. To acquire millions of shares of a stock, they need to accumulate them over a long period of time if they are to avoid binge buying, which would cause a price spike upward. When institutions spread their buying over a long period of time, they instead cause the stock to make a long-term uptrend.

So how many stocks meet the $20 million per day liquidity threshold? We found that only 28 percent of all stocks that had their IPOs from 1982 through May 2017 met this criterion for liquidity. Figure 6.3 shows that fewer than one third of all stocks are tradeable from a liquidity viewpoint as they mature and go through the I-AP.

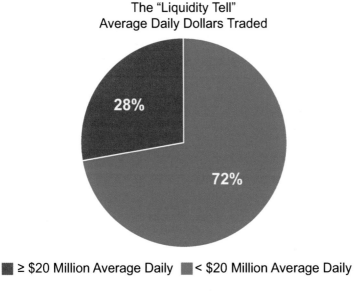

The "Liquidity Tell"
Average Daily Dollars Traded

■ ≥ $20 Million Average Daily   ■ < $20 Million Average Daily

Figure 6.3 IPO Liquidity Profile

Summary of the Key to Patience

Let's summarize the findings thus far of our study. We found that patience is key when investing in stocks right after their IPO because:

1. Few stocks make quick gains of 100 percent or more.
2. Most stocks undercut their Day 1 low price within three weeks.
3. Most stocks trigger a 10 percent stop-loss within ten weeks, even if the investor got the best price available on Day 1 of trading.
4. Stocks that do advance quickly tend to correct and give back all their profits.
5. In the long term, only 28 percent of all stocks are liquid enough to trade.

If investing in stocks were a random game with odds like these, it would seem at first glance foolish to play. This begged the question: What are the odds of finding a Super Growth Stock among the failures early in its lifecycle and profiting from it—and is it worth the search? Let's find out.

Spotting Super Growth Stocks

We have discussed several reasons why it isn't necessary to jump quickly into new stocks after they start trading. We also wondered whether there are any reasons to consider investing in stocks soon after their IPO. To answer this question, we studied how much stocks gain in their lifecycle and how many of them become Super Growth Stocks.

From the same database of stocks, we calculated the gains each stock made from their closing prices on Day 1 up to the peak price achieved (as of May 1, 2017). The findings are summarized in Figure 6.4.

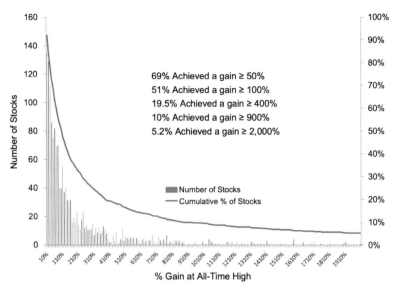

Figure 6.4 IPO Performance

The horizontal axis in Figure 6.4 shows the percent gain at the all-time high. The blue vertical bars highlight the number of stocks (shown on the left vertical axis) that achieve that level of gain. For example, more than one hundred twenty stocks achieved a gain of 0 to 10 percent at their peaks, whereas approximately forty stocks achieved gains of 100 to 110 percent. The red downward sloping line displays the percent of stocks (on the right vertical scale) that reached the level of gains at each point on the horizontal axis. For example, approximately 90 percent of all stocks achieved gains of 10 percent or more, and, as discussed earlier, 51 percent of all stocks gained 100 percent or more. We have found this to be an inverse relationship: As gains grow, the number of achievers falls.

What also can be seen in Figure 6.4 is that 33 percent of the stocks in our sample posted gains of 200 percent or more. We believe this is a large enough pool of high-performing stocks to pursue. What about the truly elite Super Growth Stocks? The ones that actually increase 900 percent or more? We found that 10 percent of all stocks gained 900 percent or more. On the far right-hand side of the chart, you can see that 5 percent of all stocks achieved astounding gains of 2,000 percent or more. We believe that gains like these are worth pursuing as it takes only one or two trades with 500 percent or more in a concentrated portfolio to change one's lifestyle. Finding the right stocks and buying and selling them at the right times in their lifecycles is difficult but still possible.

It should not be too surprising that only 10 percent of stocks achieve gains of 900 percent or more. Most everything in life has this characteristic. For example, in most industries, one or two companies dominate market share and earn most of the total profit.[11] In sports such as professional golf and tennis, only a small percentage of players worldwide are good enough to make the pro tour. Of these elite athletes, the tournament winners at Wimbledon, for example, make twice the amount of the second-place finisher and 10 times the amount of the person who loses in the quarterfinals. In the U.S. Open golf tournament, the winner also makes twice the second-place finisher and 10 times the amount of the tenth-place finisher. In entertainment, a few movie stars and singers make millions of dollars per movie or concert tour while most others need a separate steady job to support themselves.

The trading profession is no different. Most stock trades won't produce large gains—and many will be stopped-out for a loss. A small number of select trades can be highly profitable and make up for the losses in a portfolio and account for most of the profits. For a large gain, the stock must be purchased at the optimal time in its lifecycle and then handled properly with the right sell rule at the right time. We believe that the possibility of making life-changing returns makes the pursuit worth it.

---

[11]The Pareto Principle argues that 20 percent of activity produces 80 percent of the effects. This so-called 80/20 Rule can be found in many walks of life. For instance, in some industries, 20 percent of the companies produce 80 percent of the profits.

The trick is to identify which stocks will become Super Growth Stocks. The only way to find those stocks is to research them early in their lifecycles and identify the companies that create, dominate, and lead in their space. We are looking for the transformational companies that have strong sales growth and the catalysts for future growth. These are the type of companies that institutions become interested in; as those institutions build positions in those stocks, liquidity increases.

Over time, with great discipline, we will end up buying a few Super Growth Stocks that produce long-term gains because we will be watching for these factors. In some cases, we can trade these emerging leaders during the IPO-AP using short-term rules and become more familiar with their trading patterns as they move through the lifecycle phases.

The Liquidity Tell

Earlier in the chapter, we discussed liquidity, noting that $20 million per day is a solid benchmark for liquidity. During our study, we noticed that many of the stocks that met this liquidity threshold also ended up being the best Super Growth Stocks of the past four decades. This was a light-bulb moment: Few stocks end up being liquid enough for us to consider trading them in the long-term. The stocks that meet our liquidity benchmark have a much higher chance of being Super Growth Stocks. In fact, the data show that of the 33 percent of stocks that gain 200 percent or more, 58 percent of them pass the liquidity threshold. As was shown above in Figure 6.3, only 28 percent of all the stocks in the study met the liquidity threshold. This means that a stock that meets the liquidity threshold is roughly twice as likely (58 percent vs. 28 percent) to gain 200 percent or more than the general population of stocks.

When we review the highlights from our study of IPOs debuting between 1982–May 2017, our analysis reveals the following important findings:[12]

- 20 percent of IPOs gain 100 percent or more within their first year.
- 6 percent of IPOs gain 100 percent or more within thirteen weeks.
- 1.7 percent of IPOs gain 100 percent within thirty days, or approximately one IPO per year.
- 11 percent of all IPOs hit their all-time high within ten days and never go higher.
- 55 percent of all IPOs undercut their Day 1 price low within three weeks.
- 50 percent of IPOs undercut their Day 1 price low by at least 10 percent within nine weeks.
- 72 percent of all IPOs that gain 100 percent in six months or less give back all their gains within the next year.
- 33 percent of stocks achieve gains of 200 percent or more.
- 10 percent of stocks achieve gains of 900 percent or more.
- 28 percent of stocks trade $20 million or more in volume per day over the long run. Of these stocks, 75 percent gain 100 percent or more.
- Stocks that trade $20 million or more per day are twice as likely to gain 200 percent or more.
- Stocks that gain 100 percent in ninety days or less are twice as likely to gain 500 percent or more.
- 51 percent of stocks eventually gain 100 percent or more. Of these stocks, only 3.2 percent do not undercut their Day 1 close before gaining 100 percent.

---

[12]Only includes stocks still traded as of May 2017.

- 91 percent of stocks eventually undercut their Day 1 price low.

What does all of this mean? Few stocks post large gains right away, so in general it means that traders need to be patient. If we see a stock that breaks out from a well-formed base in the IPO-AP, we can trade it using rules designed to harvest quick gains before the stock corrects.

For transformative companies that do not have a tradeable IPO-AP, it's important to monitor the stock's trading volume. If the liquidity is greater than $20 million per day, look for the I-DDP to finish and wait for the I-AP to begin. This strategy does not guarantee success; based on our research, however, it does increase the likelihood of finding a Super Growth Stock. Then, with proper money management and the proper execution of good sell rules, we can look forward to holding a high-performing stock for a lifecycle trade.

CHAPTER 7
STOCK SELECTION AND TRADE MANAGEMENT

KNOWING THAT ONLY A FEW STOCKS will turn into Super Growth Stocks, it pays to be highly selective. We don't want to buy just any stock; we want to buy the elite performers. As a result of our study, we have developed some guidelines to follow when it comes to trade selection and management:

- **Be highly selective in trading.** Look for transformative companies with growing revenues setting up in higher probability lifecycle patterns and phases. Many IPOs can have long I-DDPs that likely will wear out or shakeout most investors. For longer holding periods, it's frequently best to be patient and wait for that first mature base. In addition, being selective and offensive in trading the IPO-AP can result in capturing fast moves, as well as possibly in establishing an early position in a Stair Stepper or a rare Rocket Ship.

- **Trade IPOs with sufficient liquidity.** As mentioned in Chapter 6, we are looking for the liquidity tell. Such trades should be attempted only in stocks trading with sufficient average daily dollar volume in order to avoid getting trapped in a position during which, when trying to sell shares, those sales dramatically affect stock price.

Volatility can destroy a stock portfolio in a hurry. If there isn't enough volume to get out of a position, the losses can become even worse.

- **Monitor recent new issues for buy points.** These entry points might include IPO bases or initial bases for the IPO-AP. We know from our study that this will be a shorter-term trade. We also monitor the first and second mature base breakouts for the I-AP (after the I-DDP) as well as breakaway gaps for either phase. As for this type of trade, we know from our study that this has the potential for a longer-term trade that could last anywhere from a few months to two years or even longer.

Where do we find stocks to trade that are setting up in IPO-AP and I-AP? We screen to look for the cream of the crop—i.e., hopefully, the next Super Growth Stock. Next up, let's run some screens to try to find big winners early.

Screening for Super Growth Stocks

Big, winning stocks don't come around every day. Super Growth Stocks are rare. In his classic book, *One Up on Wall Street*, Peter Lynch discusses finding those stocks that have the potential for big moves—*ten-baggers* as he called them. Remember, only 10 percent of IPOs enjoy this elite status, so don't expect to latch on to one very often.

With that, it's important to run regular screens of newer issues that have gone public over the past several years in order to catch stocks as they are about to enter the lucrative I-AP phase and to identify IPOs that are more likely to become Super Growth Stocks. We regularly run three screens.

The first screen, which we call *IPO Alert*, identifies new issues (within the past three years) that are trading 25 percent or more above recent 52-Week lows with average daily dollar volume of at least $20 million. We look for stocks forming IPO bases and initial bases as well as stocks that have completed the I-DDP and may be setting up a first mature base. Keep in mind that the *relative strength* of these stocks (i.e., the price move of a stock compared to all stocks in market) might be lower due to a long I-DDP correction and basing period or to a short trading history. The screen yields a mix of stocks early in their run and which may have completed I-DDPs. This way, we catch emerging stocks and are able to trade the IPO-AP, if there is one, or the I-AP.

The second screen, *Rare Jewels*, identifies new issues with strong revenue growth that have staged gains of more than 100 percent in ninety days or fewer. This screen can flag strong growth stocks that have the potential to move much higher over time. As we saw in the data analysis in the previous chapter, stocks of this caliber can go on to make gains of 500 percent or more. The potential is there, so we want to make sure they are on our radar.

The third screen, *Liquidity Matters*, identifies recent IPOs with strong revenue growth that have a high level of average daily dollar volume since the results show that liquidity matters. The minimum liquidity benchmark we used for the data analysis was $20 million per day. This might not be enough for certain traders. Some of our team members use $40 million or more per day, depending on position size.

One of our team members likes to run an additional screen of IPOs by year for the past three to four years—like a catch-all screen as usually there are not many IPOs every year. If the additional liquidity filter is thrown in, it's a quick review just to make sure nothing is missed in the past few years.

In summary, we found that it's critical to maintain a screening system and watchlist to keep track of IPOs to catch the next Super Growth Stocks. We've found success in finding emerging growth stocks that are potentially ready to start the I-AP by looking for these factors: increasing daily dollar trading volume; a price that is at least 25 percent above a long-term low; strong revenue growth; and a first mature base forming (see Figure 7.1).

Figure 7.1 Screening IPOs for Super Growth Stocks

CHAPTER 8
MONEY MANAGEMENT

WITH ANY INVESTING, whether short-term or long-term, money management and risk management are crucial. A trader can't trade if she doesn't stay in the game. The first rule of trading is that you have to practice risk management if you intend to preserve capital. Then comes making money—not the other way around. Stocks with increased volatility can quickly hurt or even destroy a portfolio unless extreme discipline is used for *position sizing* and the proper use of stop-losses. Our research has led us to develop rules for trading IPOs and Super Growth Stocks:

- **Trade only one recent IPO at a time and reduce position size to limit loss.** For example, if a full position size for a mature stock is 10 percent of equity, limit the IPO position size to no more than 5 percent of equity. If, however, the IPO is liquid and has stellar fundamentals, the full position may be warranted.

- **Buy the initial position and don't add to it, particularly during the IPO-AP.** Don't risk raising the average cost too high by adding to a position as the stock advances and increasing the odds of being stopped-out due to the volatile nature of early lifecycle stocks. We like to call this method of initiating positions *Buy Once and Sit Still* (BOSS).

- **Sell a portion of the position into strength.** We do this in order to limit the drawdown while holding through consolidations. It's easy to get carried away in the euphoria as the stock price soars. History shows, however, that parabolic moves usually end badly and that growth-stock corrections can be brutal. Keep in mind that many (not all, e.g., Google, eBay) IPOs often round-trip their initial advance; hence, following offensive sell rules or selling into strength tends to be more effective.

- **Choose a sell rule based on the lifecycle phase and pattern of the stock.** Does the stock's chart resemble one of the lifecycle patterns? Is the stock in the IPO-AP or I-AP? Knowing the phase and pattern of a stock helps to determine which sell rules to use. It's crucial to determine specific sell rules in advance in order to keep emotions out of the trade.

- **Set stop-losses.** In order to manage risk, set stop-losses for IPOs at no more than 10 percent below purchase price (wider than for mature stocks) in order to reduce the odds of being stopped-out of a newer issue (due to intraday volatility). Size the position to limit the loss to no more than 1 percent of capital; note, however, that truly exceptional traders, such as Peter Brandt, keep their average loss per trade under 0.4 percent of equity, and they attribute setting tight stop-losses as a contributing factor to their long-term success.

- **Trade IPOs only in a strong bull market.** This is worth repeating. We trade IPOs only when the market is in a bull market advance and the portfolio is doing well. We've noted this rule last; however, it is one of the most important (and expanding upon it easily could fill an entire other book!). We do not fight the market trend.

Our research has shown that following these rules and being highly selective can help one successfully trade IPOs and Super Growth Stocks. It's important to have a sound methodology, establish trading rules, and maintain the discipline to stick to those rules. Remember that the first rule of trading stocks is to preserve physical capital. But a trader also must maintain the proper mindset and psychology to be successful. Traders must not let losses destroy the confidence they need to follow their buy and sell rules at the proper times.

Mental Capital Preservation

Successful traders are calm, confident investors who sleep well at night. So important is a trader's mental state that none other than Jesse Livermore, one of the greatest traders of all time, said that preserving mental capital is more important than preserving physical capital. We call this *mental capital preservation* (MCP).

MCP is about drawing a line in the sand that indicates when to sell a position, because in order to preserve a positive state of mind for the next trade, a trader is not willing to give back any more profits. MCP is what drives a trader to determine the minimum percentage of profits to retain when holding a leading stock for a bigger move.

We developed the *MCP Holding Method* for this exact purpose (see Figure 8.1). The MCP Holding Method is used to determine the minimum percentage of profits to retain while holding a leading stock for a bigger move. For example, if at the peak price a position has $100,000 in profit and the trader refuses to give back any more than $55,000, the MCP is 45 percent (depicted by the yellow star in Figure 8.1). Said another way, the trader wants to retain at least 45 percent of the unrealized peak profits or $45,000 while attempting to hold a position for a larger move.

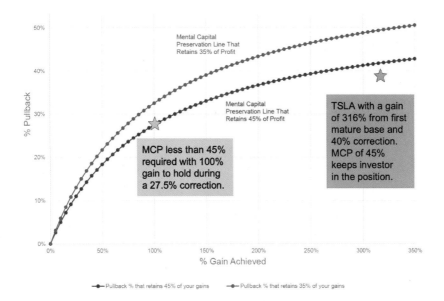

Figure 8.1 MCP Holding Method

We found that applying the MCP Holding Method is more effective after the I-DDP and at the start of the I-AP because the stock generally is less volatile during this time and the potential for long-term gains is greater. During the IPO-AP, the stock is generally too volatile to apply this method. Once past the turbulence zone, setting an MCP stop in accordance with a trader's risk tolerance will limit profit drawdowns.

How to Calculate an MCP Stop

The formula for calculating an MCP stop is:

Buy Price + (Peak Price-Buy Price) x (MCP/100)

The first step is to calculate the peak unrealized profits by taking the peak stock price minus the buy price per share. Multiply this number by the percent of peak profits to be retained. For an MCP of 40 percent, multiply by 0.40. Add this figure to your buy price. The result is your MCP stop price. If the stock trades below the MCP stop price, it triggers a sell signal; otherwise, hold the position. As the stock achieves new highs, adjust the MCP stop accordingly.

For example, if a stock were bought at $20 a share and it ran up to $50, to retain 40 percent of the peak profits (or MCP of 40 percent) the MCP stop price would be calculated as follows: $20 + ($50-$20) x (40/100) = $32

The MCP Holding Method would have a trader hold until the stock traded below $32. The MCP percent is chosen by the trader based on how much of peak unrealized profits he wants to retain while holding for a potential larger gain.

MCP Holding Method

Sitting through corrections is difficult, especially if market indexes are not behaving well. A trader needs a surprisingly large percent gain from the buy point, or cushion as we like to call it, if he is going to preserve mental capital. When market conditions are unfavorable, growth stocks can correct far more than the general market indices, making it difficult to hold a stock. For example, it's possible for a stock to decline 50 percent or more while the general market might correct only 10 to 20 percent.

We have learned that the profit and drawdown math for holding stocks for big moves is quite surprising and definitely not intuitive. Let's look at the calculation. For instance, if we asked how much profit would be retained once a gain of 100 percent was achieved on a stock, then held as the stock corrected 50 percent, what would the answer be? A trader might assume half the profits would be retained. Wrong! Let's say 10,000 shares of a stock were bought at $20. The stock went up 100 percent, trading at $40 and giving a profit of $200,000. If the stock corrects 50 percent (or .50 x $40), it will fall to $20 a share, losing the entire gain. Whether you call it a round-trip or breaking even, it wipes out all the unrealized profits. The large drawdown is mentally challenging to overcome. Table 8.1 is used to help us manage the inevitable pullback with different profit levels.

Table 8.1 Using MCP to Manage Drawdowns

% Gain Achieved	% Pullback Withstood to Retain 45% Profits (45% MCP Line)	% Pullback Withstood to Retain 35% Profits (35% MCP Line)
50%	18.3%	21.7%
100%	27.5%	32.5%
150%	33.0%	39.0%
200%	36.7%	43.3%
250%	39.3%	46.4%
300%	41.3%	48.8%
350%	42.8%	50.6%

Setting MCP stop levels and deciding when to hold positions during basing periods isn't just about determining percentages of profits and losses. It also needs to take a trader's personality into consideration: How much in unrealized profits is a trader willing to give back? How much volatility can a trader withstand? How much trading risk is a trader comfortable with? For how long can a trader endure a decline and still sleep at night?

Some traders are not willing to endure the 42.8 percent pullback and retain only 45 percent of profits after being up 350 percent (as shown in Table 8.1). However, some investors may be willing to withstand this type of pullback in an attempt to participate in a potentially larger move up.

For example, if someone had bought Tesla after the I-DDP and had a gain of 316 percent, an MCP of 45 percent would have kept the investor in the position during the 40 percent correction in the stock in late 2013 (depicted by the blue star in Figure 8.1). The investor might believe that the company is not an ordinary company, but a transformative company changing the way people drive. The investor might be looking for life-changing gains and so is willing to risk the drawdown of her unrealized profits in case the stock is able to advance higher from here. If the investor is wrong, and the stock instead moves lower, she has drawn a line in the sand using an MCP stop that will limit her drawdown. Figure 8.2 uses Tesla as an example to demonstrate a full lifecycle trade, including the initial IPO-AP, an I-DDP, and into an I-AP with the turbulence zone. We illustrated where the lifecycle sell rules we developed might work best along with MCP stops to consider for the long-term move. Let's break it down.

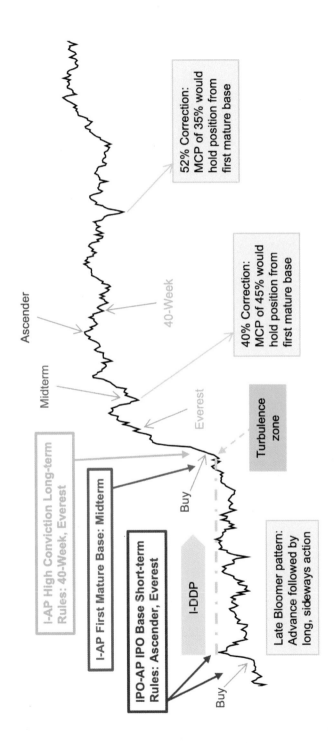

The Lifecycle Trade: Tesla   IPO 6-29-2010

Weekly Chart

I-AP High Conviction Long-term
Rules: 40-Week, Everest

I-AP First Mature Base: Midterm

IPO-AP IPO Base Short-term
Rules: Ascender, Everest

I-DDP

Late Bloomer pattern:
Advance followed by
long, sideways action

Ascender

Midterm

40-Week

Everest

Turbulence
zone

Buy

Buy

52% Correction:
MCP of 35% would
hold position from
first mature base

40% Correction:
MCP of 45% would
hold position from
first mature base

Chart Courtesy of TradeStation®

Figure 8.2 The Lifecycle Trade

In the example shown in Figure 8.2, if a trader bought Tesla at the first mature base breakout (at a cost basis of $46.68) and subsequently experienced the eventual 40 percent correction from the prior peak of $194.50 (to $116.10), an MCP of 45 percent would have kept her in the position. If a trader held the position through to the next significant correction of 52 percent from the prior peak of $291.42 (to $141.05), an MCP of 35 percent would be sufficient to prevent being stopped-out.

Because every trader has his or her own level of risk tolerance for drawdowns, we each handle MCP differently; however, our sample of the elite Super Growth Stocks has shown that a trader must be willing to accept drawdowns as high as 65 percent of peak profits (or MCP of 35 percent) in a trade to attempt to hold for a majority of the move. Traders not willing to accept such severe drawdowns can set tighter MCP stops based on their trading personality and ability to withstand drawdowns (with a tradeoff of possibly selling too early).

A note of caution: Set the MCP stop too tight and you might get shaken out of a big winner too early. Try to hold through a base or a significant correction without enough cushion in a position, and you will quickly find yourself round-tripping all the profits. Set the MCP stop too loose, on the other hand, and you might be forced to withstand large drawdowns off the peak in order to participate in a big move, and possibly risk a greater loss.

Regularly setting MCP stops like these, in conjunction with using the proper sell rules based on a stock's phase and pattern, can help manage trading risk. Remember, though, that the first rule of trading is to preserve capital: Before anything else happens, a trader has to first manage her money if she wants to live to trade another day. There's an old trader saying that says stocks take the stairs on the way up and the elevator on the way down. Setting—and sticking to—some of these key rules can help create an advantage when it comes to trading. We call it the lifecycle advantage, and we'll look at that next.

CHAPTER 9
THE LIFECYCLE ADVANTAGE

THE SUPER GROWTH STOCK STUDY we conducted sought to recognize possible edges that would identify high-performing growth stocks early in their lifecycle and suggest whether a stock might be worth trying to hold for a bigger move. Our results from the data analysis indicate that stocks that make fast gains of 100 percent or more are twice as likely to go on for much higher gains of 500 percent or more over time. However, the study also shows that many IPOs undercut their first day trading low within three weeks and that just 10 percent of IPO stocks gain 900 percent or more.

Keeping these odds in mind, the study findings made clear what it takes to hold a Super Growth Stock for a big move, such as a ten-bagger or more: An investor has to be willing to give back a significant portion of profits at various points as the stock is correcting so as to not get shaken out of the next Amazon or Tesla. What we found is that the only way to land a rare ten-bagger is to hold the stock until it closes below the 40-Week SMA (using the 40-Week Rule) or, in select cases, using the Everest Rule (for stocks that exhibit a parabolic move). It's also crucial to be able to withstand brutal drawdowns during corrections. Depending on a trader's timeframe, personality, and drawdown tolerance, setting an MCP stop or selling into strength can help do that, even if a trader holds a Rocket Ship pattern.

When a trader finds themselves in a Super Growth Stock with a rare Rocket Ship pattern, the study shows the Ascender Rule to be the second most profitable, after the 40-Week Rule, but with a lower drawdown. Taking partial profits into strength and holding on to a portion of the Rocket Ship pattern position during the IPO-AP phase might be more profitable; however, it's important to draw a line in the sand using an MCP stop in case the stock begins to round-trip as in the case of One-Hit Wonder patterns.

MCP stops help with volatility, which typically is high for early lifecycle stocks. Our research shows that volatility typically decreases after a stock moves past the turbulence zone. By that point, the stock should settle down and not be quite as volatile as in its infancy. Our experience has shown that once a position is established in the IPO-AP, it is best to not add into the position since this will raise the average cost. Therefore, an initial buy into the stock would be made, and no others, applying the sell rule and stop-loss rule only when triggered. Phasing into a position dramatically increases the odds of getting stopped-out, particularly for early lifecycle stocks and volatile new issues.

However, having said that, a set of offensive sell rules, such as Ascender or Everest, or tight MCP stops, can help to capitalize on the quick and powerful moves from IPO bases and initial bases. Our research shows that it's more lucrative in most cases to be more offensive in selling during the IPO-AP by taking profits into strength or shortly after a powerful move that reverses.

LIVES of Super Growth Stocks

After several years of research, we found that there is no holy grail for finding the next Amazon, although there is a methodology that can give us the power *to be*. The power to be individual traders, each with a unique trading style armed with the knowledge of the lifecycle trade. We believe that this methodology, when applied properly, has enhanced our trading.

To make it easy to remember the methodology to discover big winners early, think of the lifecycle, or the *LIVES*, of Super Growth Stocks. Below, we summarize key points the team took away from the study:

- **Lifecycle Phases:** A stock has a lifecycle with three distinct phases. Both of the two advance phases (IPO-AP and I-AP) can be traded; the third phase (I-DDP) is a watch phase. We believe that knowing where a stock is in its lifecycle is crucial to successfully trading stocks soon after their IPO.

- **IPO Lifecycle Patterns:** We discovered six distinct lifecycle patterns: Late Bloomers, Pump and Dumps, Stair Steppers, Rocket Ships, One-Hit Wonders, and Disappointments. We believe that early identification of the lifecycle pattern is critical to applying effective trading rules.

- **Volume:** We know from our research data that liquidity matters. We screen early in a stock's lifecycle for increasing liquidity as well as for stocks that trade a high level of average daily dollar volume.

- **Exceptional Companies.** We look for disruptive, transformative companies that are years ahead of their competition with big growth drivers. Our study underscores the importance of selectivity. Super Growth Stocks are rare jewels.

- **Sell Rules:** We use sell rules so that we can trade another day. We use a combination of sell rules (Ascender, Everest, Midterm, 40-Week) and MCP stops that fits both our trading personalities and the point at which the stock is in its lifecycle. We never risk more than 1 percent of capital. We trade early lifecycle stocks when the market is in an uptrend and our portfolios are doing well.

Even if a trader latches onto a Super Growth Stock, it would be difficult to find a rule that keeps an investor in a stock from its IPO to the ultimate peak without incurring some gut-wrenching drawdowns. Using one of the lifecycle sell rules can help in holding a high-performing growth stock for a long-term move and possibly land a ten-bagger. Just take a look at Figure 9.1. A stock can take many paths to becoming a Super Growth Stock. eBay, for example, skyrocketed from its IPO base. Google and Amazon stair-stepped their way up. Palo Alto Networks and Tesla wore out impatient investors before becoming big winners. Facebook and Netflix nose-dived before starting powerful advances. No one knows how a stock will perform, but recognizing lifecycle phases and patterns and using appropriate sell rules can give traders an edge.

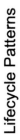

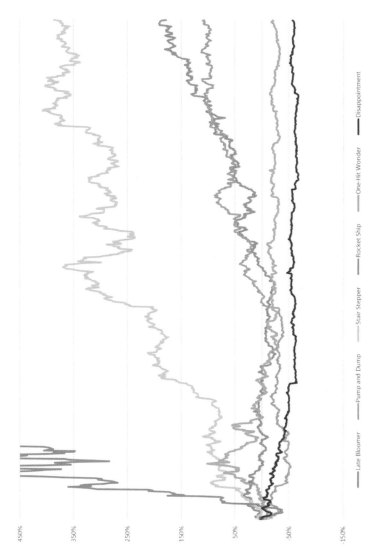

Figure 9.1 Super Growth Stock Lifecycle Patterns

What's even more exciting is that there always will be new, innovative companies that turn into leading IPOs. Entrepreneurs are always working to come up with the next revolutionary product. We can't even imagine how we ever lived without our smartphones. Already, artificial intelligence, autonomous driving, and other technologies are beginning to transform entire industries and the way we live our lives. Keep an eye out for these transformers. The next big winner may go public to much fanfare like Facebook or to generally negative sentiment as in the case of Google; regardless we will be prepared. Through our research, we now understand that the paths to success are apparent in the lifecycle phases and patterns. Because of that, we are ready to handle the next Amazon with our LIVES methodology. Just one Super Growth Stock handled well could turn into a life-changing lifecycle trade.

CHAPTER 10
A CHAT WITH THE
RESEARCH TEAM

In these pages, we've looked at how our research helped us find answers to questions we had about trading IPOs and Super Growth Stocks. We investigated whether there was an edge to trade—and profit from—the next Amazon. We looked into whether lifecycle phases, patterns, and sell rules could provide some kind of advantage. And we examined ways to avoid some of the pitfalls of trading stocks early in their lifecycle.

Our Super Growth Stock Study did, in fact, reveal answers to those questions, uncovering, among other things, strategies for navigating peaks and valleys. We also learned strategies to spot and profit from the various lifecycle inflection points of stocks. And we identified different lifecycle patterns that have helped us enhance our trades.

Now that we've come to the end of our journey, we wanted to highlight a few takeaways. In this chapter, the Super Growth Stock Study team shares some insight in an informal Q&A format.

IPO Study Journey and Takeaways

Question—What are the key takeaways from the Super Growth Stocks study?

Answer—Eric: I am convinced there is no way to identify which stocks will be big, winning stocks before their IPO simply by analyzing fundamental data of the company, including sales and earnings growth, financial ratios, information about company officers, etc. The reasons are many. Most important among them is that there are no common fundamental factors that make it clear which stocks will be wildly successful.

Eve: Eric summed it up well when we were talking about our study results: "There is no holy grail!" Other than a rare IPO like Google in 2004, it's not possible to identify in advance with a high level of certainty which IPOs will go on to become the greatest stocks; however, it is possible to make life-changing gains by picking just one Super Growth Stock early in its lifecycle and handling it well.

Kathy: IPO trades require rigorous rules and discipline. Early lifecycle stocks are usually very volatile, and a trader must be ready to buy back and sell quickly.

Kurt: The overwhelming majority of issues going public, with rare exceptions, go through the same defined price pattern process caused by the transition in ownership from the founders, angel investors, and venture capitalists to the institutional investment community. Understanding this ownership transition process is the key to using proper money management and position sizing to achieve maximum profitability.

How We Trade Now

Question—What is your trading style, and how has the study changed the way you look at and trade stocks?

Answer—Eric: I like to hold stocks for big, longer-term moves. I prefer to hold positions for four to six months. Occasionally, a few stocks are held over a year. It really depends on the market conditions. Most of the time, the market doesn't produce a long-term uptrend that allows me to hold stocks for a year or longer. Short-term corrections occur two or three times a year, making my individual stocks drop enough that I sell some stocks to limit the drawdown or losses in my portfolio. During the short-term corrections, I try to hang on to the best one to three stocks and sell my worst-performing stocks. Often, I'll buy put spreads on my best individual stocks to protect against large drawdowns and use this as protection to keep me invested in these leaders. If I stay invested more than a year in the leaders, I lock in long-term capital gains tax treatment, which makes a huge difference in portfolio growth.

Most of my losing trades are held for a much shorter time period. I find that if I have invested at the wrong time in a stock, I'm usually shaken out in less than four weeks.

After the study, I am more skeptical now of trading stocks in their early trading life as I realize how many stocks do not race right out of the gate after their debut and run up to big gains. It was eye-opening to see how many stocks make short-term gains only to quickly give them back. Most stocks fall back into the first day's trading range or, in many cases, undercut the first day's range. I learned that you don't have to be worried about missing out on big gains as few IPO stocks make large moves right from the start without having a correction or forming a base pattern.

Eve: I like to trade early stage stocks. I'm searching for the next Rocket Ship; often these moves start with a powerful breakaway gap. I have little tolerance for a stock that does not quickly show a profit. If it languishes or, even worse, starts turning negative, I sell the stock. By keeping average losses low, I can attempt a position in a stock several times while controlling risk.

In studying the Super Growth Stocks early in the lifecycle, I noticed that great timing on entries and low-cost basis are critical so as not to be shaken out of a big winner. When I take a position in a newer issue, I now rarely add to my position on the way up. Also, I watch for sell signals near the IPO's *lock-up period* expiration (usually around ninety days). Some (not all) high-flying IPOs will get hit once the lock-up expires or a couple of weeks beforehand.

I study the daily chart when trading IPO-APs. A leading new issue may correct ten days or so before rounding out and starting the right side of its IPO base, registering numerous consecutive days higher in price and closing at peak prices. Google's IPO breakout is the iconic example.

Our research made it very clear to me that many top-performing IPOs have a quick, super run and then shakeout or wear out investors. I now take profits as the stock advances for at least a portion of the position to lock in gains. I use longer-term hold rules for a small core position in a transformational company for a possible larger move when I have a significant profit. By taking some profits into strength, I can use one of the mid- to long-term sell rules (or MCP stop) from our study on the remaining position.

Kathy: As a result of our research, I have a lot more respect now for IPOs and all the stocks that I trade. I always try to remember I can't treat IPOs like mature stocks. I need to be quick to sell, but because of my trading style, that can be difficult: I like to buy at the first- and second-stage mature bases and hold for the long haul. Trading the IPO-AP is not necessarily conducive to that. This is an aspect of my trading that I am working on as a result of this study. I also must be flexible by being ready to buy back. I am more rigorous on all my trading now after having completed the study.

Kurt: New stock issues trade in two distinct phases when potentially profitable gains in price are achieved: the IPO-AP and the I-AP.

The I-AP normally occurs only when the new issue is of significant investment quality. The IPO-AP is characterized by short-lived and, quite often, rapid gains, which frequently round-trip nearly as fast and can easily turn into losses. I trade the IPO-AP with a short-term trend trade bias to take advantage of the potential profit opportunity. When a new issue makes the cut and runs in an I-AP, I typically change my speculation bias to a much longer timeframe with structured hold rules. I believe the key to taking advantage of the I-AP is proper positioning out of the first mature base. Establishing a position out of the first mature base sounds much easier than it is since standard growth stock relative price strength scanning usually will not bring the best IPO opportunities to a trader's attention at the first mature base entry price point (price strength may be lagging due to a long I-DDP).

Good and Bad IPO Trades

Question—What was one of your good IPO trades?[13]

Answer—Eric: After we finished our study, I traded Grubhub Inc. (GRUB) using the new insights I had learned. I bought the stock after it completed its I-DDP in August 2017. The stock broke out in heavy volume from its turbulence zone, and I felt like I had grabbed it at precisely the right time. However, in a few weeks, the stock shook me out most of my shares for a loss, and I sold using the Ascender Rule. In a few weeks, I bought more shares after Grubhub announced earnings and it once again broke out in heavy volume. I added more shares after the next quarterly earnings announcement when the stock broke out yet again. I held on to the shares until the overall market started to correct in early April 2018, when I sold 25 percent of the shares to limit overall portfolio risk (see Figure 10.1). The stock was up 80 percent from my initial buy when I sold those shares. At the time of this writing, I still maintain a partial position in Grubhub.

The market and stocks can act in ways that surprise us, presenting scenarios that have never happened before or we have not yet experienced. In unusual situations like these, I believe a trader must adapt. For example, Tilray (TLRY) staged a breakout after forming an IPO base and then advanced rapidly (see Figure 10.2). In fact, TLRY advanced faster than all the stocks in our database dating back to 1982.[14] Even the fastest-acting sell rule, the Everest Rule, would have been too slow to lock in sizable gains without giving back a large percentage of profits. Since TLRY was acting in an unusual fashion, I had to adapt.

---

[13]Trade examples are not intended to be demonstrative of any skills in selecting securities but instead were selected to show how IPO stocks behave. Both good and bad trades were selected based on depicting lessons learned by the authors and should not be construed as representative of performance.

[14]Delisted and acquired companies were excluded from the database.

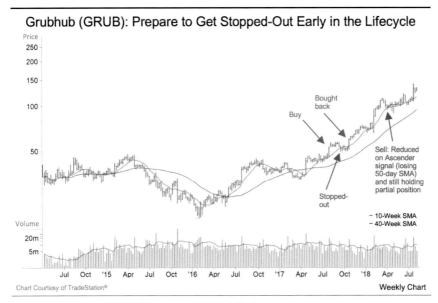

Figure 10.1 Grubhub Lesson

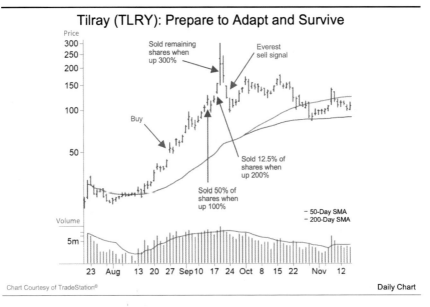

Figure 10.2 Tilray Lesson

I bought TLRY at $52.00 per share (a little late as the ideal buy point was $34.20 achieved five days earlier). TLRY kept rising and began making gains at an accelerating rate. This is called parabolic action. Eleven days after I bought, I sold 50 percent of my shares after achieving gains of 100 percent. A few days later, the stock increased even faster and kept gapping up at the open. This signaled a potential final push higher and alerted me to use discretionary selling into strength (rather than using the rules we tested in the study). I made the decision to lock in gains at 200 percent and 300 percent and, by chance, sold the remaining shares on the day the stock reached its peak price, as of this writing. Had I used the Everest Rule, I would have sold shares at a much lower price. The moral of the story: TLRY was acting in such an unprecedented fashion that I needed to adapt my behavior to the situation.

Eve: Twilio, Inc. (TWLO) was a good IPO-AP and I-AP trade. I handled the position in segments by selling a portion of it into strength and using the Ascender Rule for the rest (in case it turned out to be a huge winner). Even though I was willing to round-trip the last portion of the position—and did—the gains for the trade were significant (see Figure 10.3).

I never took the stock off my radar after selling it. TWLO subsequently went through an I-DDP and then formed a nice first mature base. Based on our research, this breakout was a buy signal and was more likely to generate a profitable move, particularly since TWLO had a successful IPO-AP in a One-Hit Wonder pattern. I bought TWLO from this first mature base and again profited from the trade, setting a sell point by using an MCP stop. I once again traded TWLO when it formed a second mature base and breakaway gap. At the time of this writing, I still hold a partial position in Twilio from the second mature base breakout.

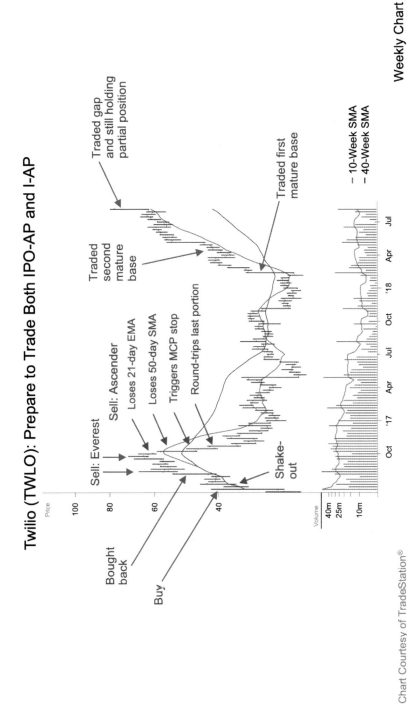

Figure 10.3 Twilio Lesson

Kathy: Acacia Communications (ACIA) was one of my best stocks. I bought successfully out of the IPO base and at a shakeout point before it really started to run. I then successfully sold it when the stock went below the 10-Week SMA. It was my best trade of the year!

I decided to purchase ACIA because it had triple-digit earnings, which is unusual for IPOs. Earnings were up 100 percent, 313 percent, and 193 percent for the last three quarters. ACIA went public in 2016, after a dry spell for IPOs. I made my first purchase on May 23, 2016, at $32.44, as it made a new high from a short IPO base (see Figure 10.4). My second purchase was on June 15, 2016, at $40.11, as it crossed a downward sloping trendline that I drew around the 10-Day SMA. I noted in my analysis on the daily chart that the high-volume blue accumulation bars dominated the red distribution bars. It was easy to hold until October 20, 2016. I sold the entire position at $95.17. My post-analysis showed that I actually should have sold the week before.

The way I handled this trade was clearly based on what I learned from the study. Normally, I'm a long-term holder, but I monitor the criteria for the Midterm Rule and for the 40-Week Rule in conjunction with an MCP of 50. For ACIA, the Midterm Rule was not violated the week before, so I did not sell. I did not know at the time that this was the IPO-AP of the stock. If I had known, I would have sold that week. Therefore, I sold it the following week as it progressed deeper below the 10-Week SMA line. I was not about to let a great trade go bad. It was a highly profitable trade, resulting in a return of 193 percent and 137 percent, respectively.

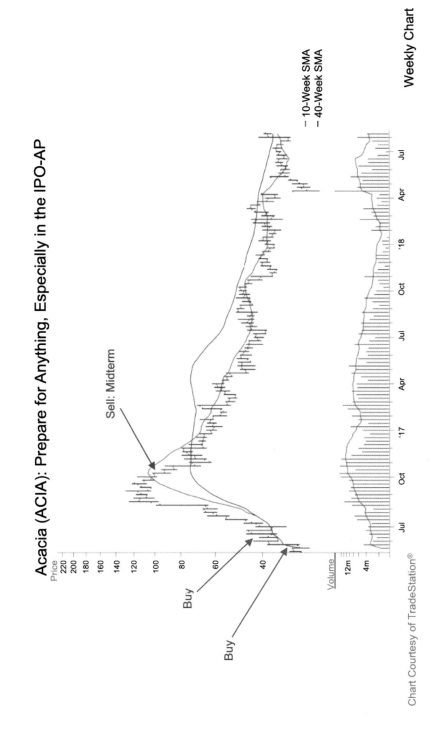

Figure 10.4 Acacia Lesson One

Kurt: Facebook (FB) was one of my best trades, although it was not traded until it had entered the I-AP. I was not aware of the lifecycle of a new issue in transition to potentially becoming a leading stock. Knowing what I do today, I think I could have had the conviction to buy a bigger stake on the July 2013 breakout, traded away one third of this stake at the intermediate top during October 2013, and purchased across the bottom, up the right side of the second mature base and at the breakout during December 2013. In actual execution, I was smaller than a full position out of the first mature base breakout and rode out the second base without taking a partial profit as the stock entered the turbulence zone. This made for an uncomfortable period in November 2013 as 66 percent of my gains at the peak melted away and I became concerned about round-tripping a 54 percent gain. I used Ajay Jani's Midterm Rule, and when it held by a fraction across the bottom of the base, I added a second position. I sequenced out a little more than half of the position, first when the Midterm Rule called a sell signal after a 1-Year hold and second when the 40-Week SMA was violated. I held a portion of the position because I set the three triggers at 3/5/7 percent below the 40-Week SMA and the 5/7 percent triggers were not hit before Facebook resumed its advance. I closed out the Facebook trade for a significant profit after holding for almost five years, on Friday March 23, 2018, near the close after it had crashed through the 40-Week SMA on enormous volume, was greater than 7 percent below the 40-Week SMA, and was almost 10 points below the 12-Month SMA without any sign of support (see Figure 10.5).

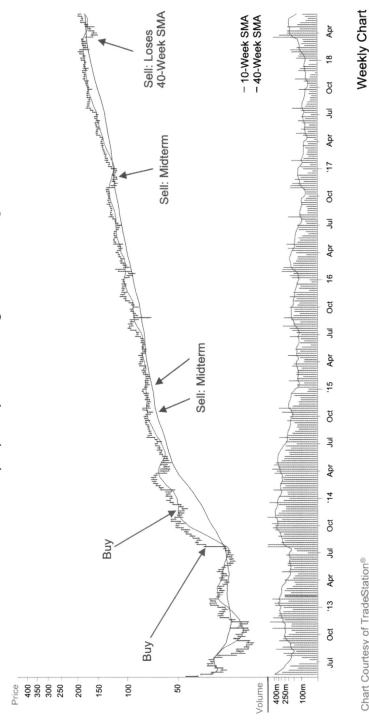

Figure 10.5 Facebook Lesson

Question—What was one of your bad IPO trades?

Answer—Eric: Two trades stand out, and both for the same reason. I missed buying both Michael Kors (KORS) and Acacia Communications (ACIA) at the proper buy points and bought them too late in the IPO-AP. Despite my late buys, they both initially were showing as profitable trades as they continued to advance.

In the KORS trade, I added shares to the winning position as the stock rose, raising my cost basis. KORS then announced a secondary share offering, and the stock made a sharp decline. I sold the stock for a much smaller gain. KORS formed another base and then broke out. I bought it again, and the stock stopped advancing. Soon after, the company announced another secondary stock offering, and the stock dropped sharply again. Again, I sold for a loss. My overall trades in KORS produced a small loss because I bought too late in the IPO-AP.

I bought ACIA late, too. After its initial debut, ACIA formed a short IPO base and then broke out and rose quickly. I missed the initial IPO base breakout and the stock made a powerful advance. A few weeks later, I bought shares too late when it made another powerful breakout (see Figure 10.6). The stock continued to advance and I had some good gains in the position. The stock started to fade, but I held on since it had not yet triggered my 10 percent stop-loss rule. The small loss quickly turned into a large loss when the stock fell sharply and went below my stop-loss target. I held on thinking it might recover some of the losses the next day. But, the stock opened sharply lower again, and I sold for much less than I could have sold the prior day. The overall trade in ACIA was a big loss, and I missed the large gains it posted in its IPO-AP.

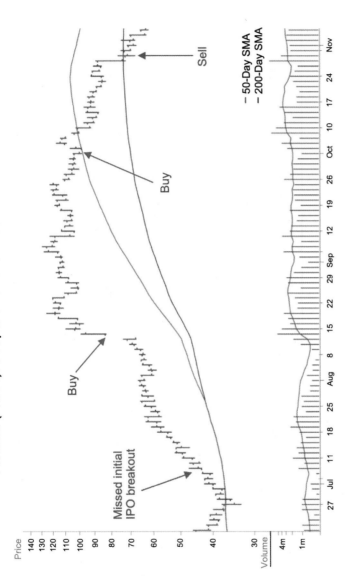

Figure 10.6 Acacia Lesson Two

Eve: I believe we learn more from our mistakes than from our winning trades. Several IPOs underscored important lessons, including Snapchat (SNAP) and Redfin (RDFN). Both stocks attempted breakouts and quickly reversed. Snapchat staged a breakaway gap on February 7, 2018, that quickly failed (see Figure 10.7). Redfin also attempted a breakout in December 2017. So far, these IPOs are Disappointments. I was stopped-out of both positions for a loss; the stocks subsequently continued much lower, showing the importance of understanding that breakouts can and do fail and proving the fact that heeding stop-loss rules is critical in case a stock turns out to be a failure.

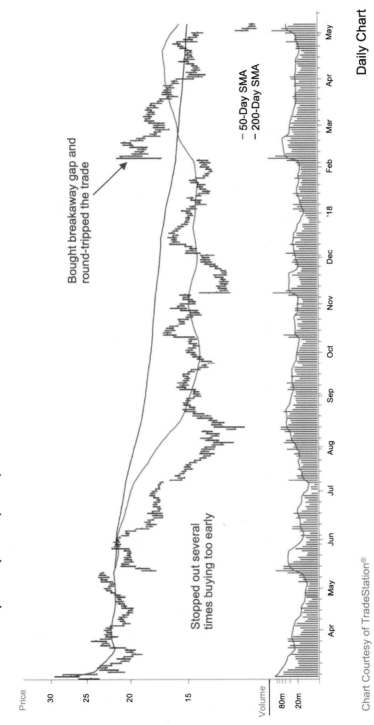

Figure 10.7 Snap Lesson

Kathy: Alibaba (BABA) was one of my worst IPO trades. I successfully bought it out of the IPO base (see Figure 10.8). When the stock initially broke the 10-Week line, I continued to hold. I was trying to use long-term rules for an IPO that was not yet a mature stock. I was thinking it would somehow gap up. I held for weeks as it lived below the 10-Week until it finally gapped down further and I had to sell everything for a significant loss.

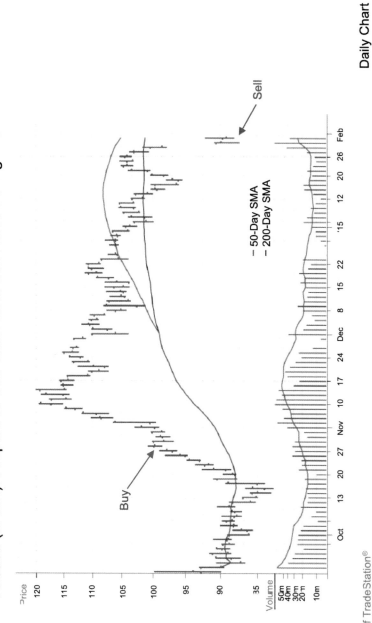

Figure 10.8 Alibaba Lesson One

Kurt: With Visa (V), I tried to use long-term hold rules when the stock was advancing shortly after trading as a public company in the IPO-AP. After showing a reasonable profit in the trade that was worth taking, Visa traded back to my buy point and I sold out. I had just paid the price for using the wrong set of rules with a new market issue. I had no idea what the lesson from this experience was other than to be thankful for not taking a loss after being up more than 10 percent. I had paid IPO cycle trading tuition and had no idea I had been to the schoolhouse, learning nothing new from the experience at the time.

Another trade shortly after, Palo Alto Networks (PANW) was trend-traded for a small gain without a clue that I was in the I-AP. This potential leading stock should have been a focus of my buy list until I was properly established out of its second mature base.

Finally, another expensive trade lesson, Alibaba (see Figure 10.9) was flawlessly entered early in the IPO-AP. When it cleared May 1 highs, I had a properly sized position with a 30 percent gain. Using a hold mindset in an attempt to repeat my success in Facebook, I once again round-tripped a gain worth having. After all these trades, I finally recognized that I had been routinely paying trade tuition with IPOs and needed to figure out what I was doing wrong.

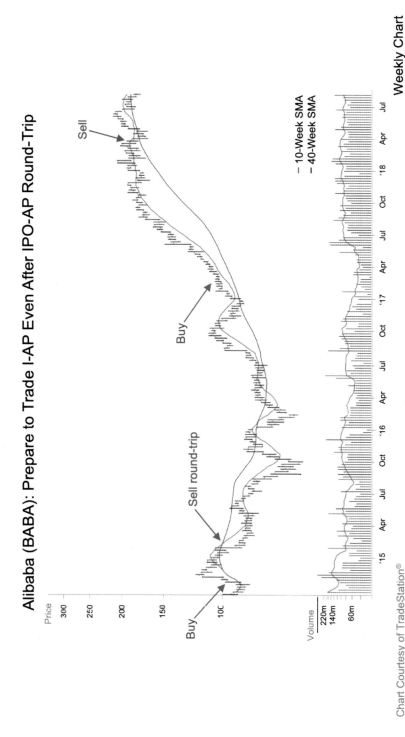

Figure 10.9 Alibaba Lesson Two

Chart Courtesy of TradeStation®

IPO Trading Insights

Question—What trading insights did you gain from the study?

Answer—Eric: I learned to be more patient. I do not trade the first day a new issue starts trading and, in most cases, I wait weeks to months. I wait for the stock to form a consolidation or base of some sort, and I then buy if it breaks out in heavy volume. I do not get too aggressive with position size as recent IPO stocks are much more volatile than mature stocks. Also, I try not add to the position as it rises: I try to BOSS.

It's easy to get excited as you see the stock running up quickly early in its lifecycle and to think you should have a bigger position in order to cash in on the stock. The trouble is, these stocks are prone to sharp sell-offs, as they have no trading history. Also, these companies tend to have secondary offerings within the first six to nine months of their initial offering. Secondary offering announcements tend to cause sharp sell-offs, as do investment analysts' upgrades and downgrades, which happen quickly and unexpectedly for recent issues.

I take smaller position sizes in recent IPOs because their volatile action can shake you out more often, as the position size makes the drawdowns unbearable. I also limit myself to owning only one recent IPO at a time for the same reasons.

Finally, I put a sell stop-loss order in at 10 percent below my purchase price. On a mature stock, I normally use a 3 to 5 percent stop-loss. For recent IPOs, when I used 3 to 5 percent, I found I was more likely to get stopped-out for a loss soon after purchasing the shares, only to frequently see the stock recover and then advance further.

Eve: Proper risk management for IPOs is critical. They can be fast, very profitable trades, however, if the position moves lower, lightning speed is needed to protect capital. I reduce position size for recent IPOs. I trade newer issues when the market is strong and the overall portfolio is doing well. For a transformative company such as Tesla, I consider holding a portion of a winning position using one of the lifecycle sell rules or the MCP Hold Method.

Kathy: I realized that I can't treat IPOs like mature stocks. They act differently, and so I need to treat them differently. I do not trade on the first day; instead, I wait for an IPO base or consolidation. If it works, I'm prepared to sell quickly if it starts to reverse. What I've found most important is to have some hard-and-fast rules written down that I absolutely will follow.

Kurt: I trend trade the IPO-AP and make a deliberate effort to take profits with offensive selling during the advance, unless the new offering exceeds an 80 to 100 percent gain in short order without a significant pullback (these situations are quite rare).

I've developed new routines and scanning processes to identify and keep track of the best new issues once they come up 25 to 30 percent off 52-Week price lows, as this is the time to conduct due diligence and trade preparation—i.e., while the first mature base process is underway.

Questions—What do you now look for in IPOs to determine if you will put on a trade? What do you look for in the technical action? Do you consider fundamentals? How do you size your IPO positions?

Answer—Eric: I first look at daily dollar trading volume and do not consider trading the stock unless it trades $10 million in daily dollar average volume, as I do not want to get caught in a position that I cannot exit quickly without moving the stock's price.

I look for a consolidation, hopefully below the high of the stock's opening-day trading range. If the stock has formed a somewhat stable consolidation and then breaks out in volume, I usually will buy. I avoid trading recent IPO stocks that have wide and loose trading patterns (or very large daily and weekly trading ranges), especially if they have been trading only a few weeks.

I consider fundamentals, and I especially like companies that already are profitable with strong sales growth rates. Occasionally, I will buy some companies that are not profitable yet. I'm more cautious and probably will buy a smaller position in such an instance.

Eve: I like to calculate the *average true range* (ATR) of a stock and size the position in an IPO based on how much more volatile it can be versus a more stable stock that has been trading for some time. I usually make the position size half (or less) of what I typically would place in a more mature stock. I'm looking for a great chart pattern and a transformative growth story. If all the numbers are there, the company is transformative, the chart pattern is great, and the stock is liquid, I may take a full position.

Kathy: If an IPO does not trade at least $40 million per day, I generally will not buy it. There are exceptions to this rule. If I were to choose to buy the stock, it would be for considerably less than the amount I would buy for a mature stock that trades more than $40 million per day. If the early stage stock has great fundamentals, I'm almost definitely in, especially if it is liquid and it has a small, tight base. I don't like to buy if it doesn't have solid fundamentals. If the company is doing something new that can change the world, I will consider it.

Kurt: I look for strong price action and liquidity. I try not to get caught in the hype both good and bad that many traders get trapped in. Strong earnings, sales, and fundamentals give me conviction in a trade's potential. Now that I understand the volatility, risk, and advance duration of the IPO-AP, I tend to size my positions smaller and adhere to short-term trend trade rules unless the initial IPO-AP advance exceeds 100 percent from a buy point.

Question—How do you find IPOs and monitor an IPO watchlist?

Answer—Eric: As I hear about stocks that are going to have an IPO, I put them on a calendar marking the day of their proposed debut. Sometimes I don't hear about them before their IPO debut. I become aware of them because of a strong price advance. In these cases, I add them to a special watchlist in my charting software labeled "Recent IPOs," and I look at their charts often in order to try to find a proper entry point.

Eve: As part of my weekly routine, I run the three IPO screens we developed as part of the study: IPO Alert, Rare Jewels, and Liquidity Matters. I scan the charts of all the new issues on these screens for strong technical action. Stocks of interest are added to my daily watchlist for further analysis and research.

Kathy: I keep a yearly IPO screen that has all the IPOs for that year, and I run through them periodically.

Kurt: I keep track of scheduled earnings reports each quarter, building a weekly list of buy candidates that have become publicly traded within the past three to five years. A new issue must have sufficient liquidity to make the cut to be on my list.

Question—How do you determine when to sell your IPO position?

Answer—Eric: I use a combination of the sell rules that we studied. I also use an MCP *stop-limit order* so that, for the IPO stocks that go up 10 percent or more, I make sure I retain half of those gains (MCP 50) by moving up my stop-loss to the price that allows me to keep half of the gains.

Eve: I look at the lifecycle phase and which of the lifecycle patterns the stock most closely resembles. I apply one of the rules that worked best for that phase and pattern in our testing, or I use an MCP stop. I frequently will sell a portion of a profitable position into strength.

If it's a transformative company early in the lifecycle, I'll usually try to hold a portion of the position for a possible larger gain since the next time I buy an eBay-like Rocket Ship breakout, I want to ride the trend.

Kathy: I like to use the moving average as support lines. If my stock breaks a support line and there is nothing for the stock to bounce off of, I usually drop it. If the stock regains the line, I will not necessarily buy it back. I will wait for a proper buy point or a new high. Then I use the moving average lines again. Depending on the character of the stock, it may be the 21-Day EMA or the 50-Day SMA; I evaluate that as necessary. I also keep active alert stops at MCP 50 and 60. All of this factors into when I sell the stock.

Kurt: I act immediately once I have round-tripped a bad trade. Unfortunately, this has been a regular occurrence for my past IPO-AP trade entries. Before our study, I never knew how common it is for price to undercut a proper IPO base entry point. I am now focused on using short-term offensive sell rules in the IPO-AP and long-term rules once the I-AP gets underway.

Question—How do you control emotions and the stress of trading highly volatile IPOs?

Answer—Eric: Our study has helped me keep my emotions in check as I am now more aware of what typical IPO action is versus atypical action. Also, by trading in smaller position sizes and only one IPO at a time, it's much easier to handle the stress of these volatile positions.

Kathy: In general, I manage stress with twice-daily meditation and plenty of sleep. I have noticed that when I am well rested and have had my daily meditations, life is much calmer, relaxing, and joyful, so my stock market decision-making does not affect me one way or the other because I know I followed my rules and I can always buy a stock back. The key is consistency.

Kurt: I use hard stops, trying to keep emotions out of it. For the initial IPO advance, I know I need to incorporate more aggressive stops for offensive profits. My focus needs to change to taking partial profits on peaks earlier because in well over 90 percent of the IPO-APs observed, profit opportunities are short-lived and tend to round-trip in a big hurry.

Eve: Reducing the position size for volatile IPOs helps me stick to the rules. I use rules to take emotion out of trading. On weekends, I document a plan for each position. When I've been holding a stock for a while and the technical action signals a pullback, I occasionally will reduce the position or buy put options to protect the position. This helps me hang on during more severe pullbacks.

I start each day by meditating to help me feel centered, calm, and focused. After meditating, I practice yoga and spend time biking, running, or swimming. I work hard to maintain a healthy lifestyle; I feel it has a positive impact on my trading. I make it a point to allocate time to enjoy interests beyond the stock market to keep myself balanced. I have a great group of friends I travel with and spend time with. I also undertake annual stock market retreats during which I get away from it all—including the market. This allows time to study and reflect since successful trading is rooted in a trader's mental state. In his book *Trading Psychology 2.0*, Dr. Brett Steenbarger argues that "successful trading has to fit into your life, not the reverse." I have found these useful words to live by.

Afterword
by Brett N. Steenbarger, Ph.D.

In these pages, you have learned from the authors how they go about finding Super Growth Stocks—those elusive "next Amazon" stocks. An important idea conveyed by Boboch, Donnelly, Krull, and Daill is that these stocks follow a lifecycle pattern from IPO infancy through maturation. Understanding where a stock is in its lifecycle provides important clues as to how to trade and invest.

I say trade and invest because the lifecycle trade is relevant to both shorter-term traders and longer-term investors. One of the outstanding observations I've made in studying active traders is that what they trade is just as important as how they trade. Mike Bellafiore of SMB Capital and author of *The Playbook* describes "stocks in play": those that display unusual movement and relative volume due to catalysts. At points in the lifecycle, Super Growth Stocks are likely to be in play—and not just for a day or two. That creates meaningful day-to-day trading opportunities. For the investor, of course, Super Growth Stocks offer a way to beat the market by participating in the growth of these companies and the trends that result.

In the final chapter, the chat with the research team, you can see that taking advantage of Super Growth Stocks is more complicated than simply putting your money in the next hot IPO. The team describes IPO watchlists and various criteria to monitor, from fundamental indications of growth to volume traded. Having a basket of potential Super Growth Stocks for investment—i.e., constructing a true growth portfolio—allows the math to work in our favor. Even if only a few of our companies achieve Super Growth Stock status, their gains can easily exceed the losses on the shares that stall out. That right-hand tail of investment returns is a powerful aid for money managers—financially and psychologically.

In his excellent book *Thinking, Fast and Slow*, Daniel Kahneman distinguishes two information processing systems in the brain. One is rapid and engages in real-time pattern recognition. The other is deep and slow and engages in deliberation and analysis. Fast thinking is the domain of the trader, picking up patterns that tell us when market flows are reversing or extending. Slower, deeper thinking is the domain of the investor, guiding idea generation, structuring of positions, and construction of portfolios. As I discuss in the book *Trading Psychology 2.0*, an important component of success in financial markets is playing to one's cognitive (information processing) strengths. Whether you succeed by trading or investing in Super Growth Stocks will hinge upon your skills at pattern recognition and/or your talents for rigorous and unique analysis.

Note that both deep and rapid thought require the capacity to sustain focus, as well as the ability to see parts and assemble them into wholes. This is why success in financial markets requires a high degree of creativity in perception and thought. Superior pattern recognition and superior depth of analysis allow the successful money manager to see and act upon what is not apparent to others.

This is where psychology becomes so relevant to market success. If we are caught up in fears and fantasies regarding our profits and losses, we no longer sustain concentration and creative synthesis and we lose our ability to find those unique, promising ideas and manage them in sound, rules-based ways. I am currently writing a book on spirituality and its relationship to money management. A core idea of the new text is that success in achieving and sustaining creative insight requires an ability to transcend the ego. A major challenge of focusing on Super Growth Stocks is not getting our egos caught up in our own super growth. Turning trading and investing best practices into rules-based processes is a great way to ensure that we are making decisions for the right reasons.

The answer to so many psychological challenges in trading and investing boils down to knowing oneself. As the authors make clear in these pages, the path to achieving Super Growth Stock status, even for the most promising companies, is not a straight line higher. Many times, these stocks trade with meaningful volatility, which means that meaningful corrections can occur along the way to solid returns. My research finds that market participants, as a function of personality traits, have differing tolerances for risk. Many successful portfolio managers who I work with spend significant time structuring their trades and constructing their portfolios to create favorable reward relative to risk—and to take as much volatility and drama out of the equity curve as possible. It's not enough to know the characteristics of Super Growth Stocks; you also have to know yourself, how you best manage money, and how you can leverage your strengths to best exploit these growth opportunities.

I wish you well in this endeavor. Ultimately, successful money management pushes us to refine ourselves: to maximize our strengths, minimize weaknesses, and find the motivations beyond the push and pull of ego that can sustain a happy and fulfilling career. Done right, improving ourselves as traders requires us to improve our selves. That is a noble challenge that can fuel our own super growth!

Appendix I
Key Terms

Ascender Rule: A partially offensive sell rule for the IPO-AP that sells a position in portions at the break of the 21-Day EMA, 50-Day SMA and holds the last portion for a potential larger profit based on time or percent price gain.

average true range (ATR): A measure of volatility that shows how much a stock moves (i.e., the range from price high to low) over a particular time frame. This measure can be used to help set stop-loss points. For example, a new IPO likely will have a high ATR and require a wider stop-loss (and, hence, a smaller position size).

base or consolidation: A stock's sideways move (usually for several months or longer), with a defined upper and lower price range between which the stock trades.

breakaway gap: When a stock jumps in price over a defined consolidation, opening and closing significantly higher than the prior day's close, which can indicate the start of a new trend.

breakout: When a stock's price moves decisively outside a defined consolidation or resistance level, typically with increased volume.

Buy Once and Sit Still (BOSS): A method of establishing an initial position and not adding as the stock advances to prevent raising the average cost too high.

consolidation or base: A stock's sideways move (usually for several months or longer), with a defined upper and lower price range between which the stock trades.

cushion: The percent gain from a stock's buy point that gives an investor the ability to withstand a pullback and still be profitable in a trade.

defensive sell rule: Taking profits in a stock when it has broken a prior uptrend in order to preserve any remaining unrealized gains.

Disappointment: A lifecycle pattern characterized by an almost immediate downtrend from its public debut and rarely starts an I-AP.

Everest Rule: An offensive sell rule for both the IPO-AP and I-AP that sets a tight (one- to two-day) trailing stop after a parabolic move.

iconic stocks or iconic Super Growth Stocks: Famous examples of high-performing growth stocks.

initial base: A base greater than seven weeks from the IPO start date (prior to I-DDP).

Initial Public Offering (IPO): The first time the stock of a private company is offered to the public.

Institutional Advance Phase (I-AP): The price advance out of a mature base after a consolidation or Institutional Due Diligence Phase (I-DDP).

Institutional Due Diligence Phase (I-DDP): A long, sideways-to-down consolidation process (over the course of months to years) after the completion of the IPO Advance Phase (IPO-AP) or IPO Advance Failure (IPO-AF).

IPO Advance Failure (IPO-AF): A stock that does not have an IPO-AP or that round-trips the entire IPO-AP.

IPO Advance Phase (IPO-AP): This is the initial advance of an IPO.

IPO Alert: This screen identifies new issues (within the last three years) that are trading 25 percent or more above recent (52-Week) lows with average daily dollar volume of at least $20 million.

IPO base: A short consolidation within seven weeks of the IPO start date.

IPO disease: When an IPO stock immediately round-trips gains or never makes any significant gains.

Late Bloomer: A lifecycle pattern characterized by a long I-DDP phase prior to an I-AP.

lifecycle patterns: Defined price patterns formed by newly public companies throughout their lifecycle from IPO to mature stock. The six unique patterns we discovered are Late Bloomers, One-Hit Wonders/One-Hit Wonders Plus, Rocket Ships, Pump and Dumps, Stair Steppers, and Disappointments.

lifecycle phases: Defined periods of price movement from IPO to mature stock.

lifecycle sell rules: Sell rules (i.e., Ascender, Midterm, 40-Week, and Everest) the research team used in the study to test IPOs and Super Growth Stocks.

lifecycle trade: A method for trading stocks throughout their lifecycle phases and patterns.

liquidity: The degree to which a stock can be quickly bought or sold in the market without affecting the stock's price. A typical gauge for liquidity can be derived by taking the number of shares traded per day times the closing price of the stock.

Liquidity Matters: This screen identifies new issues (within the last three years) that have a minimum average daily dollar volume of $20 million, along with strong revenue growth of at least 50 percent in the last quarter.

LIVES: A methodology the study team developed for trading IPOs and Super Growth Stocks based on their research results.

lock-up period: A contractual restriction that prevents insiders and shareholders who hold the company stock before going public from selling their shares for a period of time after the stock goes public.

mature base: A base that occurs after the I-DDP phase.

MCP Holding Method: A method to determine the minimum percentage of profits to retain while holding a leading stock for a bigger move.

mental capital preservation (MCP): Preserving a positive state of mind for the next trade.

Midterm Rule: A defensive sell rule for a stock's I-AP that sells on a significant undercut of the second week below the 10-Week SMA, among other sell signals.

offensive selling or offensive sell rule: Taking profits in a stock when it has made a significant advance in order to lock in gains while the stock is exhibiting strength.

One-Hit Wonder: A lifecycle pattern categorized by a fast IPO-AP followed by an undercut of the rally and possibly the entire IPO base structure.

One-Hit Wonder Plus: A One-Hit Wonder that completes a I-DDP phase and stages a mature base breakout proceeding to an I-AP.

parabolic move: An exponential rise in a stock in which the angle of ascent increases.

percent of peak profit retained: The percent of profits retained from the buy point to the peak stock price while holding the position to the sell rule exit price.

position sizing: The dollar amount that an investor is going to allocate per trade.

Pump and Dump: A lifecycle pattern characterized by the stock starting to tank soon after its IPO, and consolidates for several months to a year or more before starting its move up.

Rare Jewels: This screen identifies new issues (within the last three years) that staged gains of more than 100 percent in ninety days or fewer. Stocks that make this screen must also have an average daily dollar volume of at least $20 million and strong revenue growth of at least 50 percent in the last quarter.

relative strength: A ratio of stock price performance as compared to a market average, generally the S&P 500.

Rocket Ship: A lifecycle pattern characterized by an explosive upward move during the IPO-AP.

round-trip: Having a gain in a stock and allowing the stock to fall back to a break-even or initial buy point, essentially wiping out all unrealized profits.

secondary offerings: The post-market sale of shares with proceeds going to insider sellers rather than the issuing company.

Stair Stepper: A lifecycle pattern characterized by successive consolidations and breakouts while never undercutting the IPO base.

stop-limit order: An order to execute a trade at a specified price or better after a stop price is triggered.

stop-loss rule: The maximum amount of initial capital invested a trader is willing to lose on a new position.

stopped-out: When a stop-loss is triggered and a stock is sold for a loss.

Super Growth Stocks: Stocks that have proven themselves to be exceptionally lucrative investments (increasing 100 to 900 percent or more) in transformative companies with accelerating growth.

Super Growth Stock Lifecycle: The mapping of phases and patterns from IPO to Super Growth Stock.

ten-bagger: A stock that rises to ten-times its initial buy price. The term was coined in the book *One Up On Wall Street* by Peter Lynch.

trailing stop: A stop order that automatically adjusts to the current market price of a stock.

turbulence zone: A prior high area creating resistance and a temporary ceiling on the stock chart, usually at the end of the I-DDP.

40-Week Rule: A defensive sell rule for a stock's I-AP that sells on an undercut of the 40-Week SMA.

Appendix II
Resources for Trading

How Legendary Traders Made Millions by John Boik

Lessons from the Greatest Stock Traders of All Time by John Boik

Diary of a Professional Commodity Trader by Peter L. Brandt

Trend Following by Michael W. Covel

How I Made $2,000,000 in the Stock Market by Nicholas Darvas

Trading in the Zone by Mark Douglas

How Charts Can Help You in the Stock Market by William L. Jiler

Reminiscences of a Stock Operator by Edwin Lefèvre

One Up on Wall Street by Peter Lynch with John Rothchild

Momentum Masters by Mark Minervini, David Ryan, Dan Zanger, and Mark Ritchie II

Finding the Next Starbucks by Michael Moe

How to Make Money in Stocks by William J. O'Neil

Hedge Fund Market Wizards by Jack D. Schwager

Market Wizards by Jack D. Schwager

How to Make Money in Stocks Success Stories by Amy Smith

Trading Psychology 2.0: From Best Practices to Best Processes by Brett N. Steenbarger

www.chartpattern.com by Daniel J. Zanger

Index

Bold page numbers indicate glossary entries. Page numbers followed by *f* or *t* represent *figures* and *tables*. Footnotes are signified by the letter n.

Made in the USA
Columbia, SC
28 August 2021